Low Carb
Sinfully
Delicious
Desserts

Low Carb Sinfully Delicious Desserts

VICTOR KLINE

healthylivingbooks

New York • London

Healthy Living Books
Hatherleigh Press
5-22 46th Avenue, Suite 200
Long Island City, NY 11101
www.healthylivingbooks.com

Library of Congress Cataloging-in-Publication Data

Kline, Victor.
  Low carb sinfully delicious desserts / Victor Kline.
      p. cm.
  Includes bibliographical references and index.
  ISBN 1-57826-199-6 (alk. paper)
  1. Low-carbohydrate diet—Recipes. 2. Desserts. I. Title.
  RM237.73.K565 2005
  641.5'6383—dc22
                                                2005002305

All Healthy Living Books titles are available for bulk purchase, special promotions, and premiums. For more information, please contact our Special Sales Department at 1-800-528-2550.

Cover design by Dana Sloan
Interior design by Eugenie Delaney and Deborah Miller

Printed in Canada
10 9 8 7 6 5 4 3 2 1

Acknowledgements

I would first like to thank God for giving me all the gifts that life has to offer.

Thank you, Andrew Flach, for giving me this awesome opportunity with Hatherleigh Press and believing in me. You are making my dream a reality.

Thank you to the entire team of Hatherleigh Press for all your hard work and dedication and many long hours spent on this project. A special thank you to Kevin, Andrea, and Alyssa.

Thank you, Misty, Victoria, and Jerome, you guys are my world.

Mom, even though your time was cut short on this earth, you were always there for me.

Eric, got you last!!!

Thank you, Emeril (Food Network chef), you are a true inspiration.

Levi Wayne (author of *Wisemen: The Awakening*), never give up your dream. Thank you for your friendship.

And most of all, to all my fans, both diabetics and low carb dieters, thank you for all your nice letters and emails. I hope you enjoy eating these desserts as much as I did creating them.

Contents

Introduction: Cake, Love, and Happiness   xi

1 COOKIES AND BARS   1

Chocolate Chip Cookies	2
Raspberry Wafer Cookies	4
Peanut Butter Cookies	5
Almond Delight Spritz Cookies	6
Macaroon Cookies	7
Almond Spring Cookies	8
Pecan Sandies	9
Pecan Macaroons	10
Piña Colada Tea Cookies	11
Sugar Cookies	12
Walnut Cookies	13
Victoria's Chews	14
Peanut Butter Patties	15
Low Carb Peanut Butter Bars	16
Low Carb Chocolate Protein Bars	17
Low Carb Cinnamon Bars	18
Low Carb Protein Bars	19
Lemon Meringue Bars	20
Macadamia Nut Cheese Cookies	21
Hazelnut Mini Diamonds	22

2 CAKES AND MUFFINS   23

Pound Cake   24

Banana Cake   25

Chocolate Cake Supreme   26

Coffee Cake Delight   27

Almond Whisper Cake   28

Sour Cream Occasion Cake   29

Chocolate Peanut Butter Cake   30

Pumpkin Pudding Cakes   31

Pumpkin Spice Cake with Cream Cheese Frosting   32

Blueberry Muffins   34

Faux Bran Muffins   35

Davenport Lemon Sponge   36

Chocolate Lovers Sponge   37

3 CHEESECAKES   38

Bake-Free Cherry Cheesecake   39

New York Style Cheesecake   40

Pumpkin Cheesecake   42

Strawberry Cheesecake   44

Peanut Butter Cheesecake   46

Strawberry Key Lime Cheesecake   48

Quick Plain Cheesecake   50

Quick Plain Chocolate Cheesecake   51

Autumn Cheesecake   52

Chocolate Cheesecake   54

Chocolate Orange Cheesecake   56

Caramel Pecan Cheesecake   58

4 PIES AND TARTS   59

Silk Peanut Butter Pie	60
Pumpkin Pie Dessert Cups	62
Chocolate Crème Pie	63
Butterscotch Crème Pie	64
Vanilla Crème Pie	66
Berry Coconut Crème Pie	67
Strawberry Crème Pie	68
Custard Pecan Pie	70
Macadamia Vanilla Cheese Pie	72
Pumpkin Pecan Pie	74
Chocolate Pecan le Torte	75
Chocolate Torte	76
Vanilla Praline Pecan Torte	77
Eggnog Cheesecake Tart with Chocolate Crust	78

5 CUSTARDS, FLAN, AND MOUSSE   80

Tiramisù	81
White Chocolate Mousse Trifle	82
Egg Custard	83
Spanish Flan	84
Chocolate Spanish Flan	85
Banana Spanish Flan	86
Lemon Crème Mousse	87
Raspberry Crème Mousse	88
Banana Mousse Supreme	89
Almond Mousse	90
Oreo Mousse	91
Tapioca	92
White Chocolate Crème Mousse	93
White Berry Cream Dessert	94
Eggnog Mousse	95
Chocolate Cream Custard	96

Bread Pudding   97
Crème Brûlée   98

6 FUDGE, CHOCOLATE, AND CANDY   99

Guilt-Free Fudge   100
Nutty Peanut Butter Fudge   101
White Chocolate Fudge Dreams   102
Little Boo's Brownies   103
Brownie Bites   104
Chocolate Meal Shake   105
Peanut Butter Cup Poppers   106
Chocolate Frozen Drops   107
Cream Cheese Chocolate Squares   108
Peanut Butter Squares   109
Chocolate Raspberry Truffles   110
Hazelnut Truffle Bites   111
Cocoa Peanut Butter Truffles   112
Mint Chocolate Delights   113
Peanut Butter Delights   114
Cherry Squares   115
Macadamia Nut Chocolate Melt-A-Ways   116
Cappuccino Hazelnut Candy   117
Chocolate Doughnut Fritters   118
Coconut Peanut Butter Truffles   119
Chocolate Coconut Crunch Cups   120
Chocolate Joles   121

7 ICE CREAM AND FROZEN TREATS   122

Simple Vanilla Ice Cream   123
Strawberry Ice Cream   124
Blueberry Ice Cream   125
Cinnamon Ice Cream   126

Chocolate Ice Cream   127

Peanut Butter Ice Cream   128

Banana Ice Cream   129

Frozen Chocolatesicles   130

e8° **TOPPINGS AND FROSTING**   **131**

Chocolate Topping   132

Vanilla Frosting for Cakes or Cupcakes   133

Chocolate Frosting for Cakes or Cupcakes   134

Dipping Chocolate   135

Appendix A: Glossary   136

Appendix B: Calculating Carbohydrates   146

Appendix C: Substitutions and Measurements   148

Index   152

Cake, Love, and Happiness

Whether you are trying to cut your sugar intake, are on a low carb diet, or are a diabetic, the number one thing you have to do is stop baking with refined sugar. For years you have baked with sugar, but now it's time to use a substitute. Don't be afraid to change your baking habits. Selecting a sweetener is quite simple and the end results might surprise you as much as they surprised me.

Through many hours of searching the major grocery stores, I've come to the conclusion that there are only three main players in the artificial sweetener marketplace. There are others available, but they cannot be found outside of a specialty shop or online order. The three main artificial sweeteners are SPLENDA®, Equal, and Sweet'N Low®.

When choosing an artificial sweetener, you will have to look at many different factors to find out what works best for you. Does the sweetener leave an aftertaste? Is the conversion chart for switching your recipe from sugar to artificial sweeteners simple and not time consuming? Can you find this product easily at your local grocery store?

Another large factor is breakdown during baking. When you bake with an artificial sweetener, you need to make sure that it incorporates completely with the other ingredients, and the batter has the same consistency as it would with sugar. You also have to make sure that the artificial sweetener you choose does not separate during the baking process.

Once you have figured out which sweetener is best for you, then you are on your way to converting from your old sugar baking habits and being allowed to have your cakes and chocolates, too.

Many of us grew up looking at the little pink packets of Sweet'N Low® everywhere we went. It was on every restaurant table, every diner counter, and even at grandma's house, but we never really knew exactly what it was made of and where it came from.

First introduced in 1957, Sweet'N Low® Brand sugar substitute contains nutritive dextrose, 3.6% saccharin (36 mg per packet), cream of tartar, and calcium silicate (an anti-caking agent).

Dextrose is a natural carbohydrate derived from corn. All the sugar substitutes in powder form contain some dextrose, which is used to dilute the very potent sweetener to make it measurable for consumers.

The actual sweetener in Sweet'N Low® is saccharin, discovered in the late 1800's. It is between 300 and 500 times sweeter than sugar. There have been many concerns surrounding saccharin, but recent studies available at www.saccharin.org have proven it is safe.

The next sweetener to hit the market was Equal. Equal's sweetening ingredient is aspartame, from components commonly found in milk, meats, fruits, and vegetables. Other ingredients are added to this sweetener to make it easier to measure and pour. More information about Equal is available at www.equal.com.

Equal packets ingredients: dextose with maltodextrin, aspartame

Equal Spoonful ingredients: maltodextrin and aspartame

The third artificial sweetener on the playing field, SPLENDA®, is now widely marketed and easy to use. I personally find that the taste is almost as good as refined sugar. The conversion rate is simple from sugar to SPLENDA® and the consistency is the same with every dessert I tested. This product can be found at almost every grocery store and is now being carried at most convenient stores as well.

SPLENDA® No Calorie Sweetener contains sucralose and is made from sugar, so it tastes like sugar and has no unpleasant aftertaste. SPLENDA® can be used in cooking and baking in a variety of recipes. Like many no and low calorie sweeteners, SPLENDA® No Calorie Sweetener also contains a very small amount of the common food ingredients dextrose and/or maltodextrin for volume. Because the amount of these ingredients is so small, SPLENDA® has an insignificant calorie value per serving and meets FDA's standards for "no calorie" sweeteners.

SPLENDA® is created through a patented, multi-step process that starts with sugar and finishes with a no calorie, non-carbohydrate sweetener. The process selectively replaces three hydrogen-oxygen groups on the sugar molecule with three chlorine atoms. Chlorine is present naturally in many of the foods and beverages that we eat and drink every day, ranging from lettuce, mushrooms, and table salt. Its addition to sucrose converts it to sucralose, an exceptionally stable sweetener that tastes like sugar, without sugar's calories. After consumption, sucralose passes through the body without being broken down for energy, so it has no calories, and the body does not recognize it as a carbohydrate.

With this brief introduction to the main three artificial sweeteners, let me show the results of my dessert challenge when I put all my recipes from *Low Carb Sinfully Delicious Desserts* to the test!

CHALLENGER NUMBER ONE: Sweet'N Low®

I had all my packets and conversion charts from sugar to Sweet'N Low® spread out on my work table and with my kids by my side, we started opening all those little packets. Though the kids had fun, I felt that this was a waste of time and it was taking the fun out of baking. I noticed that the conversion from sugar to Sweet'N Low® was a bit complicated, and I also had to keep measuring this product to make sure that the sweetness was not too strong and overpowering the flavor of the dessert.

After 15 minutes of combining my ingredients and perfecting the taste, I poured my batter into a cake pan and placed it in the oven. When I pulled the cake out, I allowed it to cool for 20 minutes on a bakers rack and soon discovered that my results were not very promising. The taste was bitter and the finished product wasn't 100% what I was looking for.

With Sweet'N Low®, my cakes started to fall in the center and the outsides would crumble. I tried all different kinds of baking methods to try to correct this problem but I had no luck. I tried baking on low heat for longer periods of time, as well as high heat for shorter periods of time, and results came out the same. Once my testing ended, I came to the conclusion that this product does not work for me.

CHALLENGER NUMBER TWO: EQUAL

Once again I laid out all my ingredients on my work table and I was ready. I had both of Equals' products in front of me (Packets and Equal Spoonful) and even though the kids had their tearing hands ready for those packets, I decided to use the Equal Spoonful to make it easier on Dad. The measurements for Equal Spoonful is pretty simple; the conversion is 1 for 1 (1 cup of sugar = 1 cup of Equal Spoonful).

After mixing all the ingredients together, I tasted the cake batter and it was way too sweet. I remixed the cake batter and added the Equal a little bit at a time until the batter tasted perfect. I ended up using about 1/2 of what the conversion said on the side of the package. I love sweet desserts, but there was simply too much sweetness and it could ruin the outcome of the finished product.

I was very happy to find out that my cake didn't fall in the center and the edges were very moist. This product works very well in all my dessert recipes, but the trouble with it is you have to make sure you add the artificial sweetener to your mix a little at a time or your finished product will just taste too sweet. This can be very frustrating and time-consuming for a novice cook.

CHALLENGER NUMBER THREE: SPLENDA® SUGAR BLEND FOR BAKING

The work table was ready, the ingredients spread out and the challenge began. There were no packets to open and this made me happy. I looked at the measurements and this time it read 1 cup of sugar = 1/2 cup of SPLENDA® Sugar for Baking.

I decided to be cautious on this product because of my last challenger. I didn't want to waste any more ingredients, so once again I added the artificial sweetener as my last step to make sure that the taste wasn't going to be too sweet.

The recipe called for 2 cups of sugar, so that would come to 1 cup of SPLENDA® Sugar for Baking. I first added only 1/2 cup and tasted the batter. It needed more so I them added the other 1/2 and it tasted perfect. So far, I was very pleased with SPLENDA®. It blended well with the other ingredients and the consistency was exactly what I was looking for.

After 30 minutes, I pulled out my cake and allowed it to cool on my bakers rack for 20 minutes. I looked at the finished product and it was complete. The center held up and the edges were just right. For biggest challenge, the taste, I could not tell the difference. SPLENDA® gave me the best results in all areas. The taste was perfect, the breakdown was what I was looking for and the end result was the same as if I was using refined sugar.

My cooking tests drove me to choose to cook with SPLENDA®. I now use SPLENDA® in all my baking recipes at home and at work. I'm not saying that you shouldn't use other artificial sweeteners that are out there in the market, but that my challenge proved to me that SPLENDA® did exactly what I was looking for in an artificial sweetener.

The recipes in *Low Carb Sinfully Delicious Desserts* are designed for every possible occasion. I know that one of the biggest challenges low carb dieters and diabetics face are the holidays. With this book, not only can you have cheesecake, pies, cookies, and other mouthwatering desserts you crave, you can enjoy the eating festivities during the holidays with your family.

If you have any questions about any recipes in this book or any other questions, please feel free to contact me at LowCarbDesserts@aol.com or you can visit my web site at www.VictorKline.com. Use *Low Carb Sinfully Delicious Desserts* for all your holidays and meal planning and remember:
Cake, Love, and Happiness...

God Bless,

Victor Kline

ARTIFICIAL SWEETENER MEASUREMENT CHARTS

Sweet'N Low® SUBSTITUTION CHART

For best results, experiment by substituting half the amount of sugar in a recipe with the sweetening equivalence of Sweet'N Low®.

Sweet'N Low® Packets

1/4 cup granulated sugar	=	6 packets
1/3 cup granulated sugar	=	8 packets
1/2 cup granulated sugar	=	12 packets
1 cup granulated sugar	=	24 packets

Sweet'N Low® Bulk

1/4 cup granulated sugar	=	2 teaspoons
1/3 cup granulated sugar	=	2 1/2 teaspoons
1/2 cup granulated sugar	=	4 teaspoons
1 cup granulated sugar	=	8 teaspoons

Sweet'N Low® Liquid

1/4 cup granulated sugar	=	1 1/2 teaspoons
1/3 cup granulated sugar	=	2 teaspoons
1/2 cup granulated sugar	=	1 tablespoons
1 cup granulated sugar	=	2 tablespoons

EQUAL SUBSTITUTION CHART

Equal sweetens like sugar, but its cooking properties are different. Equal works very well in fruit pies; however, cakes, cookies and pastries depend on sugar for bulk, tenderness, and browning, properties that most sugar alternatives don't have. When baking with Equal, prolong cooking at high heat levels. This may result in some loss of sweetness.

Equal Packets

1/4 cup granulated sugar	=	6 packets
1/3 cup granulated sugar	=	8 packets

1/2 cup granulated sugar	=	12 packets
1 cup granulated sugar	=	24 packets

Equal for Recipes

1/4 cup granulated sugar	=	1 3/4 teaspoons
1/3 cup granulated sugar	=	2 1/2 teaspoons
1/2 cup granulated sugar	=	3 1/2 teaspoons
1 cup granulated sugar	=	7 1/4 teaspoons

Equal Spoonful

1/4 cup granulated sugar	=	1/4 cup
1/3 cup granulated sugar	=	1/3 cup
1/2 cup granulated sugar	=	1/2 cup
1 cup granulated sugar	=	1 cup

STEVIA SUBSTITUTION CHART

Stevia

1 cup granulated sugar	=	1/3 teaspoon

SWEETVIA SUBSTITUTION CHART

Sweetvia

1 cup granulated sugar	=	1/3 teaspoon

SWEEVIA SUBSTITUTION CHART

Sweevia

1 cup granulated sugar	=	1/3 teaspoon

SPLENDA® GRANULAR SUBSTITUTION CHART

SPLENDA® granular is my favorite sugar substitution to use. It's simple. 1 cup for 1 cup.

SPLENDA® Granular

1 cup granulated sugar	=	1 cup

SPLENDA® SUGAR BLEND SUBSTITUTION CHART

SPLENDA® Sugar Blend

1 cup granulated sugar	=	1/2 cup

1

Cookies and Bars

Chocolate Chip Cookies

Makes 24 cookies ∽ 1/2 ounce per cookie ∽
1 net carb per cookie

CHOCOLATE CHIPS

> 2 cups unsweetened cocoa powder
> 1 cup artificial sweetener
> 1/2 cup softened unsalted butter

COOKIE DOUGH

> 2 1/2 cups almond flour
> 1 1/4 cups artificial sweetener
> 1 1/2 teaspoons baking powder
> 1/4 teaspoon salt
> 1 egg
> 1 1/2 cups softened unsalted butter
> 1 teaspoon vanilla extract

CHOCOLATE CHIPS

1. Make at least 2 hours ahead or preferably 1 day before making the cookies.
2. Set the mixer to low and combine the cocoa and artificial sweetener together.
3. Add the butter and beat until well blended.
4. Place the mixture between two pieces of parchment paper and with a rolling pin, roll out until flattened.
5. Place on a small cookie sheet. Set in the freezer until hardened.

COOKIE DOUGH

1. Preheat the oven to 350 degrees Fahrenheit.

2. Set the mixer to low and combine the almond flour, artificial sweetener, baking powder, and salt together.

3. Add the butter, egg, and vanilla and beat until well blended.

4. Remove the chocolate sheet from the freezer. Using a rolling pin, break up the sheet into small pieces by rolling back and forth.

5. Using a rubber spatula, gently fold the chocolate chips into the cookie dough. Do not use a mixer for this step. If you use a mixer, the chips may melt and you will have chocolate cookie dough.

6. Using a 1/2 ounce scoop or a tablespoon, drop the dough onto a nonstick cookie sheet.

7. Bake until golden brown, approximately 8 to 10 minutes.

8. Allow the cookies to cool on the sheet on a cooling rack for 10 minutes, then transfer them to a rack to cool completely.

9. Store the cookies in a dry, airtight container.

Raspberry Wafer Cookies

Makes 36 cookies ～ 1/2 ounce per cookie ～
2.0 net carbs per cookie

> 5 tablespoons softened unsalted butter
> 5 ounces softened cream cheese
> 5 tablespoons plain or vanilla low carb protein powder
> 1/4 cup artificial sweetener
> 1 jar (14 ounces) sugar-free raspberry preserves

1. Preheat the oven to 350 degrees Fahrenheit.
2. Set the mixer to medium and combine the butter and cream cheese together. Beat until soft and fluffy.
3. Add the protein powder and artificial sweetener slowly. Don't worry if the dough starts to clump up in the beginning, just continue to beat until the dough is well blended.
4. Set the dough in a glass bowl, cover with plastic wrap, and place in the fridge for 2 to 3 hours.
5. On a piece of parchment paper, roll the dough flat (about 1/4 inch thick). Cut the dough into 2-inch squares and place them on a nonstick cookie sheet.
6. Bake the wafers until they start to brown on the edges, approximately
7 to 8 minutes.
7. Set them on a plate to cool.
8. Spread the raspberry preserve evenly on 1 wafer, then sandwich 2 wafers together. Repeat as needed.
9. You can use any flavor of sugar-free preserves.
10. Store the wafers in a dry, airtight container.

Peanut Butter Cookies

Makes 8 cookies ⌒ 1/2 ounce per cookie ⌒
1.5 net carbs per cookie

2 cups sugar-free peanut butter
1/4 cup artificial sweetener
2 eggs
1 1/2 teaspoons vanilla extract

1. Preheat the oven to 325 degrees Fahrenheit.
2. Set the mixer to medium and combine the peanut butter and artificial sweetener together. Beat until well blended.
3. Add the eggs one at a time and beat until smooth.
4. Add the vanilla and beat until well blended.
5. You can either roll the dough into a log and freeze, then cut into 1/4 inch pieces, or use 2 teaspoons to drop the dough onto a nonstick cookie tray, then flatten the dough down with a fork.
6. Bake approximately 8 to 10 minutes until the edges are golden brown.
7. Transfer to a rack to cool completely.
8. Store the cookies in a dry, airtight container.

Almond Delight Spritz Cookies

Makes 16 cookies ∽ 1/2 ounce per cookie ∽
1.5 net carbs per cookie

3 cups almond flour	1/2 cup softened unsalted butter
2 cups artificial sweetener	1 teaspoon almond extract
2 eggs	1 teaspoon vanilla extract

1. Preheat the oven to 325 degrees Fahrenheit.
2. Set the mixer to low and combine the almond flour and artificial sweetener. Beat until well blended.
3. Set the mixer to medium and add the eggs one at a time. Beat until smooth.
4. Add the butter, almond extract, and vanilla extract and beat until dough is well blended.
5. Using a 1/2 ounce scoop or a tablespoon, drop the dough onto a nonstick cookie sheet.
6. Bake the cookies until the edges are golden brown, approximately 6 to 8 minutes.
7. Transfer to a rack to cool completely.
8. Store the cookies in a dry, airtight container.

If you make these cookies during the holiday and want to sprinkle them with snow, take:

1 cup artificial sweetener
1/2 cup corn starch

1. Mix the artificial sweetener and corn starch together.
2. Using a sifter, sprinkle the mixture on the cookies to give a snow effect on top.
3. This does not change the net carb count.

Macaroon Cookies

Makes 12 cookies ~ 1/2 ounce per cookie ~
1.5 net carbs per cookie

4 egg whites
1/4 teaspoon salt
1 1/2 teaspoon vanilla extract
1 cup artificial sweetener
1/2 cup almond flour
2 cups unsweetened coconut

1. Preheat the oven to 300 degrees Fahrenheit.
2. Set the mixer on high and beat the egg whites, salt, vanilla, and artificial sweetener together until the mixture starts to form peaks. Do not overmix. If you overmix, the egg whites will become dry.
3. In a separate bowl, using a wooden spoon, combine the almond flour and the unsweetened coconut together.
4. Using a rubber spatula, fold the almond flour and unsweetened coconut mixture into the egg whites by hand. Mix until well blended.
5. Using a 1/2 ounce scoop or a tablespoon, drop the dough onto a nonstick cookie sheet.
6. Bake the cookies until golden brown, approximately 20 to 25 minutes. Try not to rush the baking process. Macaroons take a little longer to bake.
7. Allow the cookies to cool on the sheet on a cooling rack for 10 minutes. Transfer to a rack to cool completely.
8. Store the cookies in a dry, airtight container.

Almond Spring Cookies

Makes 8 cookies ∽ 1/2 ounce per cookie ∽
2.3 net carbs per cookie

> 1/4 cup softened unsalted butter
> 1 cup artificial sweetener
> 1 egg
> 1 1/2 cup almond flour
> 1/2 teaspoon almond extract

1. Preheat the oven to 325 degrees Fahrenheit.
2. Set the mixer on medium and beat the butter, artificial sweetener, egg, almond flour, and almond extract together until the dough forms a ball.
3. Remove the dough from the mixing bowl and form 8 medium sized balls. Place the balls on a nonstick cookie sheet and press them with the end of a fork for design.
4. Bake the cookies for 6 to 8 minutes.
5. Allow the cookies to cool for 30 minutes before serving.
6. Store the cookies in a dry, airtight container.

Pecan Sandies

Makes 20 cookies ⟋⟍ 1/2 ounce per cookie ⟋⟍
2.9 net carbs per cookie

1 cup softened unsalted butter
1 cup vegetable shortening
1 1/2 cups artificial sweetener
4 cups almond flour
1 teaspoon salt
1/2 teaspoon baking powder
2 large eggs
1 1/2 cups chopped pecans
1 teaspoon vanilla extract
1 cup whole pecans

1. Preheat the oven to 325 degrees Fahrenheit.
2. Set the mixer on low and combine the butter, vegetable shortening, artificial sweetener, almond flour, salt, and baking powder together. Beat until smooth.
3. Slowly add the eggs, chopped pecans, and vanilla extract and beat until the dough is well blended
4. Using a teaspoon, shape the dough into 1-inch balls and place them onto a nonstick cookie sheet.
5. Put a whole pecan on top of the cookie ball, flattening the ball slightly.
6. Bake for 15 to 18 minutes or until the edges are golden brown.
7. Allow the cookies to cool for 30 minutes before serving.
8. Store the cookies in a dry, airtight container.

Pecan Macaroons

Makes 10 macaroons ⌒ 1/2 ounce per macaroon ⌒
2.2 net carbs per macaroon ⌒ Fancy cookies add .2 net
carbs per macaroon, for a total of 2.4 net carbs

4 egg whites
1/2 teaspoon cream of tarter
3/4 cup artificial sweetener
1/4 teaspoon vanilla extract
1 1/2 cups chopped pecans

1. Preheat the oven to 350 degrees Fahrenheit.
2. Set the mixer to high and beat the egg whites and cream of tartar together until peaks form. Do not over-mix.
3. Using a rubber spatula, fold in the artificial sweetener, vanilla extract, and chopped pecans.
4. Using a teaspoon, shape the cookie dough into 1-inch balls and place them onto a nonstick cookie sheet.
5. Bake for 10 to 15 minutes or until the edges are golden brown.
6. Allow the cookies to cool for 10 minutes.
7. To make a fancy macaroon, melt some sugar-free chocolate and dip the bottom of the macaroons into the chocolate. Then place them on a sheet of wax paper that has been sprinkled with unsweetened coconut.
8. Store the macaroons in a dry, airtight container.

Piña Colada Tea Cookies

Makes 16 cookies ⌒ 1/2 ounce per cookie ⌒
2.2 net carbs per cookie

2 1/2 cups almond flour
2 1/2 cups artificial sweetener
1 1/2 teaspoons baking powder
1 cup unsweetened coconut
1/2 cup unsweetened pineapple juice
1/4 teaspoon salt
1 large egg
1 teaspoon vanilla extract
1 1/2 cup softened unsalted butter

1. Preheat the oven to 350 degrees Fahrenheit.

2. Set the mixer on low and combine the almond flour, artificial sweetener, baking powder, unsweetened coconut, unsweetened pineapple juice, and salt together. Beat until well blended.

3. Add the egg, vanilla extract, and butter and beat until the dough is well blended.

4. Using a 1/2 ounce scoop or a tablespoon, drop the dough onto a nonstick cookie sheet.

5. Bake the cookies for 8 to 10 minutes or until golden brown.

6. Allow the cookies to cool 15 minutes before serving.

7. You can add 1/2 cup unsweetened cocoa powder to make Chocolate Colada Cookies.

8. Store the cookies in a dry, airtight container.

Sugar Cookies

Makes 16 cookies ⌒ 1/2 ounce per cookie ⌒
1.5 net carbs per cookie

1/2 cup unsalted softened butter
1/2 cup shortening
1 1/4 cup artificial sweetener
2 large eggs
1 teaspoon vanilla extract
1 1/2 cups almond flour
1/4 teaspoon salt

1. Preheat the oven to 350 degrees Fahrenheit.
2. Set the mixer to medium and cream the butter and shortening together. Beat until well blended.
3. Add the artificial sweetener and beat until smooth.
4. Add the eggs and vanilla and beat until smooth.
5. Set the mixer to low and add the almond flour and salt. Beat until blended. Do not overmix.
6. Using a 1/2 ounce scoop or a tablespoon, drop the cookie dough onto a nonstick cookie sheet.
7. Bake until the edges are golden brown, approximately 6 to 8 minutes.
8. Let the cookies cool for 10 minutes before serving.
9. Store the cookies in a dry, airtight container.

Walnut Cookies

Makes 12 cookies ∽ 1/2 ounce per cookie ∽
1.75 net carbs per cookie

1 cup crushed walnuts	1/4 teaspoon salt
1 cup artificial sweetener	1 cup softened unsalted butter
1 1/2 cups of whole grain pastry flour	2 eggs
1 teaspoon baking powder	1/4 teaspoon vanilla extract

1. Prepare the cookie dough one day before you intend to bake.

2. In a medium bowl, combine the walnuts, artificial sweetener, flour, baking powder, and salt together by hand. Set aside.

3. Set the mixer to low and combine the butter, eggs, and vanilla together in a large bowl. Beat until smooth and fluffy.

4. Add the dry mixture slowly and beat until the dough is well blended. Do not overmix. The dough will be thick.

5. Roll the dough into 1-inch logs on a piece of parchment paper and refrigerate overnight.

6. The next day, preheat the oven to 300 degrees Fahrenheit.

7. Remove the logs from the fridge and cut into 1-inch pieces. Place them 2 inches apart on a nonstick cookie sheet.

8. Bake until golden brown, approximately 15 to 20 minutes.

9. Remove the cookies from the oven and flatten while warm.

10. Place the cookies back into the oven and bake for another 5 minutes.

11. Allow the cookies to cool for 10 minutes before serving.

12. Store the cookies in a dry, airtight container.

Victoria's Chews

Makes 24 chews ꝏ 3/4 ounce per serving ꝏ
2.0 net carbs per cookie

1 cup softened unsalted butter
1 cup half and half
5 cups artificial sweetener
4 tablespoons unsweetened cocoa powder
1/4 teaspoon salt
2 teaspoons vanilla extract
5 tablespoons sugar-free peanut butter
5 cups unsweetened coconut

1. Set the mixer on low and combine the butter, salt, half and half, artificial sweetener, cocoa, and salt together. Beat until well blended.

2. Pour the mixture into a medium-size saucepan and boil for 2 minutes or until it becomes smooth on low heat.

3. Remove the pan from the heat and add the vanilla, peanut butter, and coconut. Mix by hand until well blended.

4. Using a 1/2 ounce scoop or a tablespoon, drop the dough onto a piece of parchment paper.

5. Refrigerate the chews for 3 hours before serving.

6. Store the chews in the fridge.

Peanut Butter Patties

Makes 12 patties ∽ 1/2 ounce per patty ∽
2.0 net carbs per cookie

1 3/4 cups whole grain pastry
   flour

3/4 cups artificial sweetener

1/2 cup artificial brown sweetener

2 tablespoons cornstarch

1 1/2 teaspoons baking powder

1/4 teaspoon baking soda

1/4 teaspoon salt

1 cup sugar-free peanut butter
   (chunky is OK)

1/4 cup canola oil

1 egg

2 teaspoons vanilla extract

1. Preheat the oven to 350 degrees Fahrenheit.

2. In a medium bowl, using a wooden spoon, combine the whole grain pastry flour, artificial sweetener, artificial brown sweetener, cornstarch, baking powder, baking soda, and salt together and stir until blended. Set aside.

3. Set the mixer to medium and combine the peanut butter, oil, egg, and vanilla together in a large bowl. Beat until smooth.

4. Set the mixer to low and add the dry ingredients slowly. Beat until well blended. The dough will look a little bit crumbly. Do not overmix.

5. Using a 1/2 ounce scoop or a tablespoon, drop the dough onto a nonstick cookie sheet. Flatten cookies using the back of a spoon. Make sure the cookies are about 1 1/2 inches apart.

6. Bake until the cookies are golden brown, approximately 8 to 10 minutes.

7. Remove the cookies from cookie sheet and let them cool completely on a rack before serving.

8. Store the cookies in a dry, airtight container.

Low Carb Peanut Butter Bars

Makes 6 protein bars ～ 2 ounces per bar ～
2 net carbs per bar

8 ounces (8 squares) unsweetened baking chocolate
1 cup softened unsalted butter
1 1/2 cups sugar-free peanut butter
1 1/2 cups artificial sweetener
1/2 cup chopped pecans

1. In a medium saucepan, on low heat, using a wooden spoon, combine the chocolate, butter, peanut butter, artificial sweetener, and the crushed pecans together. Stir until smooth, approximately 10 minutes.

2. Pour the mixture into a nonstick loaf pan and cool on the counter for 2 hours.

3. Turn the pan over and lightly tap the bottom. Allow the loaf to fall onto a piece of parchment paper.

4. Cut into 6 pieces and wrap them in a nonstick plastic wrap.

5. Store the bars in a dry, airtight container.

Low Carb Chocolate Protein Bars

Makes 6 protein bars ⮨ 1 ounce per serving ⮨
2 net carbs per bar

4 ounces (4 squares) unsweetened baking chocolate
1 cup softened unsalted butter
2 cups chocolate protein powder
1 1/2 cups artificial sweetener

1. In a medium saucepan, on low heat, using a wooden spoon, combine the chocolate, butter, protein powder, and artificial sweetener together. Stir until smooth, approximately 10 minutes.
2. Pour the mixture into a nonstick loaf pan and cool on the counter for 2 hours.
3. Turn the pan over and lightly tap the bottom. Allow the loaf to fall onto a piece of parchment paper.
4. Cut into 6 pieces and wrap them in a nonstick plastic wrap.
5. Store the bars in a dry, airtight container.

Low Carb Cinnamon Bars

Makes 6 cinnamon bars ∽ 2 1/4 ounces per bar ∽
2 net carbs per bar

 8 ounces (8 squares) unsweetened baking chocolate
 1 cup softened unsalted butter
 1/2 cup cinnamon
 1 1/2 cups vanilla protein powder
 1/4 tablespoon nutmeg
 2 cups artificial sweetener
 1/2 cup chopped walnuts

1. In a medium saucepan, on low heat, using a wooden spoon, combine the chocolate, butter, cinnamon, protein powder, nutmeg, artificial sweetener, and walnuts together. Stir until smooth, approximately 10 minutes.

2. Pour the mixture into a nonstick loaf pan and cool on the counter for 2 hours.

3. Turn the pan over and lightly tap the bottom. Allow the loaf to fall onto a piece of parchment paper.

4. Cut into 6 pieces and wrap them in a nonstick plastic wrap.

5. Store the bars in a dry, airtight container.

Low Carb Protein Bars

Makes 8 protein bars ⌒ 1 ounce per serving ⌒
3 net carbs per bar

1/2 cup softened unsalted butter
1 cup sugar-free peanut butter
1 cup ground almonds
1 cup artificial sweetener
4 ounces dry non-dairy milk
1 teaspoon vanilla extract

1. In a medium saucepan, on low heat, using a wooden spoon, stir the butter until melted and remove from the heat. Approximately 10 minutes.

2. In the same pan, add the peanut butter, ground almonds, artificial sweetener, dry milk, and vanilla. Stir until well blended.

3. Pour the mixture into a nonstick loaf pan, cover with a nonstick plastic wrap, and freeze overnight.

4. The next day, turn the pan over and lightly tap the bottom. Allow the loaf to fall onto a piece of parchment paper. If the loaf doesn't fall out, then fill your sink with hot water and place the bottom of the pan in the hot water to allow the loaf to fall out easily.

5. Cut into 8 pieces and wrap them in a nonstick plastic wrap.

6. Store the bars in a dry, airtight container.

Lemon Meringue Bars

Makes 12 meringue bars　〰　1 ounce per serving　〰
3.6 net carbs per bar

CAKE

3 cups softened unsalted butter

4 1/2 cups almond flour

2 1/4 cups artificial sweetener

2 eggs

2 teaspoons vanilla extract

1 cup lemon juice

1/4 cup lemon extract

3 teaspoons baking powder

1/2 teaspoon salt

MERINGUE

4 egg whites

1/2 teaspoon cream of tartar

1 cup artificial sweetener

1. Preheat the oven to 375 degrees Fahrenheit.
2. Set the mixer to low and combine the butter, almond flour, artificial sweetener, eggs, vanilla extract, lemon juice, lemon extract, baking powder, and salt together. Beat until smooth. Do not overmix.
3. Scoop the batter in a 10-inch nonstick cake pan.
4. Bake for 10 to 12 minutes or until the edges are golden brown.
5. Remove the cake from the oven and place in the fridge for 1 hour.
6. While the cake is in the fridge, prepare the meringue.
7. Set the mixer on high and beat the egg whites, cream of tartar, and artificial sweetener until peaks form. Do not overmix or the meringue will become dry.
8. Remove the cake from the fridge and spread the meringue on top.
9. Cut the cake into 12 pieces.
10. Store the bars in a dry, airtight container.

Macadamia Nut Cheese Cookies

Makes 24 cookies   1/2 ounce per serving
1.8 net carbs per serving

3 tablespoons softened unsalted butter
4 ounces cream cheese
1/2 teaspoon vanilla extract
4 1/2 ounces almond flour
3/4 cup artificial sweetener
1 cup chopped macadamia nuts

1. Preheat the oven to 325 degrees Fahrenheit.
2. Set the mixer to medium and combine the butter, cream cheese, and vanilla together. Beat until smooth.
3. Add the almond flour, artificial sweetener, and macadamia nuts and beat until just blended. Do not overmix.
4. Using a 1/2 ounce scoop or a tablespoon, shape the dough into 1-inch balls. Place the balls on a nonstick cookie sheet, leaving about a 1/4 inch space between each cookie.
5. Bake for 12 to 18 minutes or until the edges are golden brown.
6. Cool for 10 minutes on a cooling rack.
7. Store the cookies in a dry, airtight container.

Hazelnut Mini Diamonds

Makes 20 mini diamonds   1/4 ounce per serving
3.0 net carbs per serving

2 cups softened unsalted butter
1 egg
1/4 teaspoon vanilla extract
3/4 cup artificial sweetener
2 cups ground hazelnuts
1 cup vanilla protein powder
1/4 teaspoon salt
1/4 tablespoon baking powder
1 teaspoon nutmeg
1/4 teaspoon cinnamon

1. Preheat the oven to 325 degrees Fahrenheit.
2. Set the mixer to medium and beat butter until smooth and light.
3. Add the egg, vanilla, and artificial sweetener and beat until well blended.
4. Set the mixer to low and add the ground hazelnuts, protein powder, salt, baking powder, nutmeg, and cinnamon. Beat until well blended.
5. Place the mixture between 2 pieces of nonstick parchment paper and roll out until flattened.
6. Place on a cookie sheet and bake for 20 to 30 minutes.
7. Remove from the oven immediately and cut into 20 square bite-sized pieces. It is best if you cut while the sheet is still warm.
8. Store the mini diamonds in a dry, airtight container.

2

Cakes and Muffins

Pound Cake

Makes 6 servings ∽ 2 ounces per serving ∽
2.0 net carbs per serving

> 2 cups almond flour
> 1 cup softened unsalted butter
> 1 1/2 cups artificial sweetener
> 5 eggs
> 1 teaspoon vanilla extract
> 1 teaspoon baking powder
> 1/4 teaspoon salt

1. Preheat the oven to 350 degrees Fahrenheit.
2. Set the mixer to medium and cream together the butter, artificial sweetener, vanilla, eggs, and salt. Beat until smooth.
3. In a separate bowl, mix the flour and baking powder together.
4. Set the mixer to low and slowly add the dry mixture to the butter mixture. Beat until the batter is smooth with no lumps.
5. Pour the batter into an 8-inch nonstick cake pan.
6. Bake for 45 to 50 minutes. Do not overbake.
7. You can add nuts to the top before baking if you desire.
8. Store the cake in a dry, airtight container.

Banana Cake

Makes 8 servings 〜 1 1/2 ounces per serving 〜
2.6 net carbs per serving

1 cup softened unsalted butter
1 1/2 cups artificial sweetener
1 teaspoon vanilla extract
1/2 cup chopped walnuts
1/4 cup banana puree
5 eggs
1/4 teaspoon salt
2 cups almond flour
1 teaspoon baking powder

1. Preheat the oven to 350 degrees Fahrenheit.
2. Set the mixer to medium and cream together the butter, artificial sweetener, vanilla, walnuts, banana puree, eggs, and salt. Beat until smooth.
3. In a separate bowl, mix the flour and baking powder together.
4. Set the mixer to low and slowly add the dry mixture to the butter mixture. Beat until the batter is smooth with no lumps.
5. Pour the batter into an 8-inch nonstick cake pan.
6. Bake for 45 to 50 minutes. Do not overbake.
7. You can add nuts to the top before baking if you desire.
8. Store the cake in a dry, airtight container.

Chocolate Cake Supreme

Makes 6 servings ⁓ﾟ 1 1/4 ounces per serving ⁓ﾟ
2.0 net carbs per
serving

  1 1/2 cups softened unsalted butter
  2 cups artificial sweetener
  1 teaspoon vanilla extract
  4 eggs
  1/4 teaspoon salt
  2 1/2 cups almond flour
  1 1/2 teaspoon baking powder
  1/2 cup unsweetened cocoa powder
  2 ounces (2 squares) unsweetened baking chocolate

1. Preheat the oven to 350 degrees Fahrenheit.
2. Set the mixer to medium and cream together the butter, artificial sweetener, vanilla, eggs, and salt. Beat until smooth.
3. In a separate bowl, mix the flour, cocoa powder, and baking powder together.
4. Set the mixer to low and slowly add the dry mixture to the butter and beat until the batter is smooth with no lumps.
5. In a microwave, melt the chocolate and add to the batter. Mix until blended.
6. Pour the batter into an 8-inch nonstick cake pan.
7. Bake for 45 for 50 minutes. Do not overbake.
8. Store in a dry, airtight container.

Coffee Cake Delight

Makes 8 servings 1 1/4 ounces per serving
3.0 net carbs per serving

1 1/2 cups softened unsalted butter
2 1/2 cups artificial sweetener
1/2 cup espresso (strong coffee also works great)
1 teaspoon vanilla extract
4 eggs
1/4 teaspoon salt
3 cups almond flour
1 teaspoon baking powder
2 ounces of unsweetened chocolate, 2 squares

1. Preheat the oven to 350 degrees Fahrenheit.
2. Set the mixer to medium and cream together the butter, artificial sweetener, espresso, vanilla, eggs, and salt. Beat until smooth.
3. In a separate bowl, mix the flour and baking powder together.
4. Set the mixer to low and slowly add the dry mixture to the butter mixture. Beat until the batter is smooth with no lumps.
5. In a microwave, melt the chocolate and add to the batter. Mix until blended.
6. Pour the batter into a 10-inch nonstick cake pan.
7. Bake for 40 to 45 minutes. Do not overbake.
8. Store in a dry, airtight container.

Almond Whisper Cake

Makes 8 servings ⌒ 1 ounce per serving ⌒
2.5 net carbs per serving

2 egg whites

6 tablespoons flaxseed meal or almond flour

4 eggs (separated)

2 teaspoons almond extract

1/4 teaspoon vanilla extract

1 1/2 cups artificial sweetener

1 cup almond flour

2 teaspoons baking powder

1. Preheat the oven to 350 degrees Fahrenheit.
2. Spray a 10-inch cake pan with a nonstick baking spray. Set aside.
3. Set the mixer to medium and whip two egg whites in a medium bowl until peaks form. Sprinkle the flaxseed meal over the egg whites, 1 tablespoon at a time. Using a spatula, fold gently after each addition to combine. Set aside.
4. Set the mixer to high and whip 4 egg whites in a large bowl until shiny and stiff. Do not overmix. Set aside.
5. Set the mixer to medium and combine the egg yolks, almond extract, and vanilla together in an another large bowl.
6. Add the flaxseed meal mixture to the egg yolk mixture and beat just until combined.
7. Add the artificial sweetener, almond flour, and baking powder. Beat for 3 minutes.
8. Using a rubber spatula, fold in the reserved beaten egg whites until smooth.
9. Pour in the batter evenly into the prepared pan. Rap pan sharply on the table to pop any bubbles.
10. Bake for 15 to 18 minutes. The cake is done when a few crumbs adhere to a toothpick when inserted in the center.
11. Remove the cake from the oven. Allow to cool in pan on a rack for 20 minutes. Run a small sharp knife between the cake and the pan edges. Flip the cake over and remove the pan.
12. Store in a dry, airtight container.

Sour Cream Occasion Cake

Makes 8 servings ∽ 1 ounce per serving ∽
3.2 net carbs per serving

1/2 cup softened unsalted butter
4 ounces softened cream cheese
2 1/2 cups artificial sweetener
2 eggs
1 tablespoon vanilla extract
1 1/2 cups sour cream
1 1/2 teaspoons baking soda
1 1/2 teaspoons baking powder
1/4 teaspoon salt
2 1/2 cups almond flour

1. Preheat the oven to 350 degrees Fahrenheit.
2. Set the mixer to medium and combine the butter, cream cheese, and artificial sweetener together. Beat until smooth.
3. Set the mixer to low and add the eggs, vanilla, sour cream, baking soda, baking powder, salt, and almond flour. Beat until well blended.
4. Scoop the batter into a 10-inch nonstick cake pan.
5. You can also add blueberries, unsweetened chocolate, or whatever else you desire.
6. Bake for 40 to 45 minutes and test with a knife. Make sure the knife comes out clean before removing from the oven.
7. Let the cake rest for 5 minutes before removing from the pan.
8. Store in a dry, airtight container.

Chocolate Peanut Butter Cake

Makes 10 servings ⌒ 3/4 ounce per serving ⌒
3.0 net carbs per serving

1 1/2 cups softened unsalted butter
2 cups vanilla protein powder
1 cup artificial sweetener
1 1/2 teaspoons baking powder
1/4 teaspoons salt
1/2 cup sugar-free peanut butter
1/2 cup unsweetened cocoa powder
1 1/2 teaspoons vanilla extract
3 eggs

1. Preheat the oven to 350 degrees Fahrenheit.
2. Set the mixer to medium and cream together the butter, protein powder, artificial sweetener, baking powder, salt, peanut butter, cocoa powder, and vanilla. Beat until well blended. The batter will be thick.
3. Add the eggs one at a time and beat until the batter is smooth.
4. Pour the batter into a 10-inch nonstick cake pan slowly.
5. Bake for 20 to 25 minutes. Check the cake using a knife. Place the knife in the center of the cake. If the knife comes out clean then the cake is ready to be removed from the oven.
6. Let the cake rest for 5 minutes before removing the cake from the pan.
7. Allow the cake to cool on a cooling rack and then store the cake in a dry, airtight container.

Pumpkin Pudding Cakes

Makes 12 servings ✑ 1/2 ounce per serving ✑
6.2 net carbs per serving

- 2 teaspoons unsalted butter
- 4 ounces cream cheese
- 1 can (7.5 ounces) pumpkin puree
- 1 cup artificial sweetener
- 2 egg yolks
- 1 egg
- 1/2 teaspoon vanilla extract
- 2 cups almond flour
- 1/2 cup heavy whipping cream
- 2 cups sugar-free whipped topping

1. Preheat the oven to 325 degrees Fahrenheit.
2. Using a double boiler, on medium heat, melt together the butter, cream cheese, pumpkin puree, artificial sweetener, egg yolks, egg, vanilla, almond flour, and cream until smooth for approximately 12 minutes. Do not boil.
3. Scoop the batter into 12 large nonstick muffin cups and bake for 15 to 25 minutes or until the knife comes out clean from the center.
4. Remove the cakes from the oven and place in the fridge for 2 hours.
5. Serve the cakes with sugar-free whipped topping.
6. Store in the fridge.

Pumpkin Spice Cake with Cream Cheese Frosting

Makes 16 servings ∾ 1 ounce per serving ∾
6.5 net carbs per serving

FROSTING

- 2 ounces cream cheese
- 1 cup artificial sweetener
- 1/2 cup softened unsalted butter
- 1/2 teaspoon vanilla extract

CAKE

- 1 can (7.5 ounces) pumpkin puree
- 3/4 cup canola oil
- 2 eggs
- 1/2 teaspoon vanilla extract
- 1/4 teaspoon salt
- 1/4 teaspoon cloves
- 1/2 teaspoon nutmeg
- 1 teaspoon cinnamon
- 1/2 teaspoon baking soda
- 1 teaspoon baking powder
- 1 1/2 cups artificial sweetener 5 tablespoons vanilla whey powder
- 1 1/2 cups almond flour

FROSTING

1. Set the mixer to medium and cream together the cream cheese, artificial sweetener, butter, and vanilla. Beat until smooth and fluffy. Cover and set aside.

CAKE

1. Preheat the oven to 350 degrees Fahrenheit.
2. Set the mixer to low, and combine the pumpkin puree, canola oil, eggs, vanilla, salt, cloves, nutmeg, cinnamon, baking soda, baking powder, artificial sweetener, whey powder, and almond flour together. Beat until well blended with no lumps.
3. Pour the batter slowly into a nonstick 10-inch cake pan.
4. Bake for 15 to 20 minutes or until the knife comes out clean.
5. Place the cake in the fridge for 4 hours.
6. Remove from the fridge and frost. Make sure you cover the sides of the cake with frosting to avoid the cake from drying out.
7. Store in the fridge until ready to serve.

Blueberry Muffins

Makes 12 muffins   ∽   1 ounce per serving   ∽
2.0 net carbs per serving

- 1 1/2 cups softened unsalted butter
- 1 cup vanilla protein powder
- 1 1/2 cups artificial sweetener
- 1 cup of flaxseed meal or almond flour
- 1 1/2 teaspoons baking powder
- 1/4 teaspoon salt
- 3 eggs
- 2 teaspoons vanilla extract
- 1 cup fresh blueberries

1. Preheat the oven to 350 degrees Fahrenheit.
2. Set the mixer to medium and cream together the butter, protein powder, artificial sweetener, flaxseed meal, baking powder, salt, eggs, vanilla, and 1 cup water until well blended.
3. Using a rubber spatula, fold the blueberries into the batter. Don't overmix or you will just have purple muffin batter.
4. Pour the batter into a nonstick muffin pan, filling the cups about 2/3 full.
5. Bake for 20 to 25 minutes.
6. Remove the muffins from the pan and store in a dry, airtight container.

Faux Bran Muffins

Makes 12 muffins   1/2 ounce per serving
2.0 net carbs per serving

1 cup unprocessed wheat bran
1 cup flaxseed meal or almond flour or wheat flour
4 1/2 teaspoons baking powder
1/4 teaspoon salt
1/2 cup artificial sweetener
3 eggs
1/2 cup heavy cream
3/4 cup half and half cream
1 1/2 teaspoons vanilla extract
3 tablespoons softened unsalted butter
1 1/2 teaspoons cinnamon

1. Preheat the oven to 375 degrees Fahrenheit.
2. Set the mixer to low and combine the wheat bran, flaxseed meal, baking powder, salt, artificial sweetener, eggs, heavy cream, half and half, vanilla, butter, and cinnamon together. Beat until well blended. The batter will be thick.
3. Using an ice cream scoop, scoop the batter into a non-stick muffin pan, filling the cups about 2/3 full.
4. Sprinkle cinnamon on top for an extra kick.
5. Bake for 15 to 20 minutes.
6. Remove from the oven and cool for 10 minutes on a rack.
7. Store the muffins in a dry, airtight container.

Davenport Lemon Sponge

Makes 12 servings ◡◠ 3/4 ounce per serving ◡◠
2.0 net carbs per serving

1 1/2 cups softened unsalted butter
1 cup vanilla protein powder
1 1/2 cups artificial sweetener
1 cup flaxseed meal or almond flour
1 cup grated lemon zest
1/2 teaspoon cinnamon
1/4 cup artificial lemon
1 1/2 teaspoons baking powder
1/4 teaspoon salt
3 eggs
2 teaspoons vanilla extract

1. Preheat the oven to 350 degrees.
2. Set the mixer to medium and cream together the butter, protein powder, artificial sweetener, flaxseed meal, lemon zest, cinnamon, artificial lemon, baking powder, salt, eggs, vanilla, and 1 cup water. Beat until well blended.
3. Pour the batter into a 10-inch nonstick cake pan, filling it about 3/4 full.
4. Bake for 20 to 25 minutes.
5. Remove from the oven and allow to cool on the counter for 15 minutes.
6. Store in a dry, airtight container.

Chocolate Lovers Sponge

Makes 12 servings ✐ 3/4 ounce per serving ✐
2.0 net carbs per serving

- 1 1/2 cups softened, unsalted butter
- 1 cup vanilla protein powder
- 3 cups artificial sweetener
- 1 cup flaxseed meal
- 1 1/2 cups unsweetened cocoa powder
- 1 1/2 teaspoons baking powder
- 1/4 teaspoon salt
- 3 eggs
- 2 teaspoons vanilla extract
- 3 ounces (3 squares) unsweetened baking chocolate

1. Preheat the oven to 350 degrees Fahrenheit.
2. Set the mixer to medium and cream together the butter, protein powder, 2 cups of the artificial sweetener, flaxseed meal, cocoa, baking powder, salt, eggs, vanilla, and 1 cup water. Beat until well blended.
3. Pour the batter into a 10-inch nonstick cake pan, filling it about 3/4 full.
4. Bake for 20 to 25 minutes. Remove from the oven and allow to cool on the counter.
5. While the cake is cooling, melt together the chocolate and 1 cup of the artificial sweetener in a microwave. Do not overcook.
6. Place the cooled cake on a large set of wax paper.
7. Pour the melted chocolate over the top and let set for 10 minutes.
8. Store in a dry, airtight container.

3

Cheesecakes

Bake-Free Cherry Cheesecake

Makes 8 servings ∽ 2 ounces per serving ∽
2.5 net carbs per serving

1 ounce box sugar-free cherry-flavored gelatin
12 ounces softened cream cheese
1 1/2 cups fat-free ricotta cheese
1 cup artificial sweetener
3/4 cups heavy cream

1. Prepare 8 small dessert bowls.
2. Boil 1 cup of water and dissolve the gelatin completely.
3. Set the mixer on high and whip the cream cheese until fluffy with no lumps.
4. Set the mixer on low and add the ricotta cheese and artificial sweetener. Beat until smooth.
5. Set the mixer to medium and add the heavy cream. Beat until thick. Do not over mix.
6. Using a rubber spatula, fold in cherry gelatin slowly until blended.
7. With a large spoon, scoop the mix into the dessert bowls and place in the fridge for 2 to 4 hours to set.
8. Store in the fridge.

New York Style Cheesecake

Makes 12 servings ∽ 4 ounces per serving ∽
3.5 net carbs per serving

CRUST

2 1/2 cups ground almonds
1/4 cup artificial sweetener
1/2 cup melted unsalted butter
1/4 teaspoon vanilla extract

FILLING

2 1/2 pounds softened cream cheese
1/2 cup sour cream
1 cup artificial sweetener
2 teaspoons vanilla extract
2 teaspoons lemon juice
1 cup heavy cream
2 egg yolks
6 eggs

CRUST:

1. No need to preheat the oven for the crust.
2. Set the mixer to low and combine together the ground almonds, vanilla extract, artificial sweetener, and melted butter. Beat until well blended.
3. Pour the crust into a 10-inch springform pan and press against the bottom and the sides.
4. Bake for 10 minutes at 350 degrees Fahrenheit.
5. Remove the crust from the oven and set aside to cool.

FILLING

1. Preheat oven to 200 degrees Fahrenheit.

2. Set the mixer to high and whip the cream cheese until fluffy with no lumps. Scrape down the sides of the bowl every 2 minutes.

3. Set the mixer to low and add the sour cream, artificial sweetener, vanilla, lemon juice, heavy cream, egg yolks, and eggs. Beat until smooth and creamy.

4. Pour the batter into the crust.

5. Bake the cheesecake for 1 1/2 hours to 2 hours.

6. Using a clean knife, check the center of the cheesecake by inserting the knife halfway through. If the knife comes out clean then the cake is ready to be removed from the oven.

7. Leave the cheesecake on a cooling rack until you can see the sides coming away from the pan. Transfer the cake to a nonstick pan and place in the fridge until served.

Pumpkin Cheesecake

Makes 12 servings ∽ 4 ounces per serving ∽
4.5 net carbs per serving

CRUST

2 1/2 cups ground almonds
1/4 teaspoon vanilla extract
1/4 cup artificial sweetener
1/2 cup melted unsalted butter

FILLING

2 1/2 pounds softened cream cheese
1/2 cup sour cream
1 can (7.5 ounces) pumpkin puree
1/2 tablespoon cinnamon
1/2 tablespoon nutmeg
1 1/2 cups artificial sweetener
1 1/2 teaspoons vanilla extract
2 teaspoons lemon juice
1 cup heavy cream
2 egg yolks
5 eggs

CRUST:

1. No need to preheat the oven for the crust.
2. Set the mixer to low and combine the ground almonds, vanilla, artificial sweetener, and melted butter together. Beat until well blended.
3. Pour the crust into a 10-inch springform pan and press against the bottom and the sides.
4. Bake for 10 minutes at 350 degrees Fahrenheit.
5. Remove the crust from the oven and set aside to cool.

FILLING

1. Preheat the oven to 200 degrees Fahrenheit.

2. Set the mixer on high and whip the cream cheese until fluffy with no lumps. Scrape down the sides of the bowl every 4 minutes.

3. Set the mixer to low and add the sour cream, pumpkin puree, cinnamon, nutmeg, artificial sweetener, vanilla, lemon juice, heavy cream, egg yolks, and eggs. Beat until smooth and creamy.

4. Pour the cheesecake batter into the crust.

5. Bake the cheesecake for 1 1/2 hours to 2 hours.

6. Using a clean knife, check the center of the cheesecake by inserting the knife halfway through. If the knife comes out clean, then the cake is ready to be removed from the oven.

7. Leave the cheesecake on a cooling rack until you can see the sides coming away from the pan. Transfer the cake on a nonstick pan and place in the fridge until served.

Strawberry Cheesecake

Makes 12 servings   4 1/2 ounces per serving
3.3 net carbs per serving

CRUST

    2 1/2 cups ground almonds
    1/4 teaspoon vanilla extract
    1/4 cup artificial sweetener
    1/2 cup melted unsalted butter

FILLING

    2 1/2 pounds softened cream cheese
    1/2 cup sour cream
    2 large cups sliced strawberries
    1 3/4 cups artificial sweetener
    1 1/2 teaspoons vanilla extract
    2 teaspoons lemon juice
    1 cup heavy cream
    2 egg yolks
    6 eggs

CRUST:

1. No need to preheat the oven for the crust.
2. Set the mixer to low and combine the almonds, vanilla, artificial sweetener, and butter together. Beat until well blended.
3. Pour the crust into a 10-inch springform pan and press against the bottom and the sides.
4. Bake for 10 minutes at 350 degrees Fahrenheit.
5. Remove the crust from the oven and set aside to cool.

FILLING

1. Preheat the oven to 200 degrees Fahrenheit.

2. Set the mixer to high and whip the cream cheese until fluffy with no lumps. Scrape down the sides of the bowl every 4 minutes.

3. Set the mixer to low and add the sour cream, 1 cup of the strawberries, artificial sweetener, vanilla, lemon juice, heavy cream, egg yolks, and eggs. Beat until smooth and creamy.

4. Pour the batter into the crust.

5. Bake the cheesecake for 1 1/2 hours to 2 hours.

6. Using a clean knife, check the center of the cheesecake by inserting the knife halfway through. If the knife comes out clean then the cake is ready to be removed from the oven.

7. Leave the cheesecake on a cooling rack until you can see the sides coming away from the pan. Transfer the cake to a nonstick pan.

8. Place the remaining sliced strawberries on top in a spiral rotation for garnish. Place in the fridge until served.

Peanut Butter Cheesecake

Makes 12 servings ⟳ 4 ounces per serving ⟳
4.0 net carbs per serving

CRUST

2 1/2 cups ground almonds
1/4 cup artificial sweetener
1/2 cup melted unsalted butter
1/4 teaspoon vanilla extract

FILLING

2 1/2 pounds softened cream cheese
1 1/2 cups sugar-free peanut butter
1/2 cup sour cream
1 3/4 cups artificial sweetener
1 1/2 teaspoons vanilla extract
2 teaspoons lemon juice
1 1/2 cups heavy cream
2 egg yolks
6 eggs

CRUST:

1. No need to preheat the oven for the crust.
2. Set the mixer to low and combine the almonds, vanilla, artificial sweetener, and melted butter together. Beat until well blended.
3. Pour the crust into a 10-inch springform pan and press against the bottom and the sides.

4. Bake for 10 minutes at 350 degrees Fahrenheit.

5. Remove the crust from the oven and set aside to cool.

FILLING

1. Preheat the oven to 200 degrees Fahrenheit.

2. Set mixer to high and whip the cream cheese until fluffy with no lumps. Scrape down the sides of the bowl every 2 minutes.

3. Set the mixer to low and add the peanut butter, sour cream, artificial sweetener, vanilla, lemon juice, heavy cream, egg yolks, and eggs. Beat until smooth and creamy.

4. Pour the batter into the crust.

5. Bake the cheesecake for 1 1/2 hours to 2 hours.

6. Using a clean knife, check the center of the cheesecake by inserting the knife halfway through. If the knife comes out clean, then the cake is ready to be removed from the oven.

7. Leave the cheesecake on a cooling rack until you can see the sides coming away from the pan. Transfer the cake to a nonstick pan and place in the fridge until served.

Strawberry Key Lime Cheesecake

Makes 12 servings ✐ 3 1/2 ounces per serving ✐
3.5 net carbs per serving

CRUST

2 1/2 cups ground almonds
1/4 teaspoon vanilla extract
1/4 cup artificial sweetener
1/2 cup melted unsalted butter

FILLING

2 1/2 pounds softened cream cheese
1/2 cup sour cream
1 3/4 cups artificial sweetener
1 1/2 cups fresh sliced strawberries
1 1/2 teaspoons vanilla extract
1 1/2 cup lime juice
1 cup heavy cream
2 egg yolks
5 eggs

CRUST

1. No need to preheat the oven for the crust.

2. Set the mixer to low and combine the almonds, vanilla, artificial sweetener, and melted butter together. Beat until well blended.

3. Pour the crust into a 10-inch springform pan and press against the bottom and the sides.

4. Bake for 10 minutes at 350 degrees Fahrenheit.

5. Remove from the oven and set aside to cool.

FILLING

1. Preheat the oven to 200 degrees Fahrenheit.

2. Set the mixer to high and whip the cream cheese until fluffy with no lumps. Scrape down the sides of the bowl every 4 minutes.

3. Set the mixer to low and add the sour cream, artificial sweetener, strawberries, vanilla, lime juice, heavy cream, egg yolks, and eggs. Beat until smooth and creamy.

4. Pour the batter into the crust.

5. Bake the cheesecake for 1 1/2 hours to 2 hours.

6. Using a clean knife, check the center of the cheesecake by inserting the knife halfway through. If the knife comes out clean, then the cake is ready to be removed from the oven.

7. Leave the cheesecake on a cooling rack until you can see the sides coming away from the pan. Transfer the cake to a nonstick pan and place in the fridge until served.

Quick Plain Cheesecake

Makes 8 servings ⌒ 2 3/4 ounces per serving ⌒
2.0 net carbs per slice

1 pound softened cream cheese
3 eggs
1 1/2 cups sour cream
1/2 cup heavy cream
1 teaspoon vanilla extract
1 tablespoon lemon juice
3/4 cup artificial sweetener

1. Preheat the oven to 350 degrees.
2. Set the mixer to high and whip cream cheese and eggs together until it becomes fluffy with no lumps.
3. Set the mixer to low and add the sour cream, heavy cream, vanilla, lemon juice, and artificial sweetener. Beat until smooth.
4. Pour the batter into a 10-inch glass pie dish.
5. Using the water bath method, place the glass dish inside the water bath and bake for 50 minutes. Make sure the water is not overflowing into the cheesecake.
6. Remove from the oven and let the cheesecake sit for 10 to 20 minutes until it reaches room temperature.
7. Place in the fridge for 1 hour before serving.

Quick Plain Chocolate Cheesecake

Makes 8 servings ✺ 3 ounces per serving ✺
2.0 net carbs per slice

1 pound softened cream cheese
3 eggs
1 1/2 cups sour cream
1/2 cup heavy cream
1 teaspoon vanilla extract
1 tablespoon lemon juice
3/4 cup artificial sweetener
3/4 cup unsweetened cocoa powder

1. Preheat the oven to 350 degrees Fahrenheit.
2. Set the mixer to high and whip the cream cheese and eggs together until fluffy with no lumps.
3. Set the mixer to low and add the sour cream, heavy cream, vanilla, lemon juice, and artificial sweetener. Beat until smooth.
4. Add the cocoa and beat until well blended.
5. Pour the batter into a 10-inch glass pie dish.
6. Using the water bath method, place the glass dish inside the water bath and bake for 50 minutes. Make sure the water is not overflowing into the cheesecake.
7. Remove from oven and let the cheesecake sit for 10 to 20 minutes until it reaches room temperature.
8. Place in the fridge for 1 hour before serving.

Autumn Cheesecake

Makes 24 servings ⌒ 4 1/2 ounces per serving ⌒
5.4 net carbs per serving

CRUST

2 1/2 cups ground almonds
1/4 cup artificial sweetener
1/2 cup melted unsalted butter
1/4 teaspoon vanilla extract

FILLING

2 pounds softened cream cheese
1 can (15 ounces) pumpkin puree
2 cups artificial sweetener
1/4 teaspoon vanilla extract
1 cup heavy whipping cream
6 large eggs
1 1/2 cups almond flour
1 teaspoon cinnamon
2 teaspoons nutmeg
1/2 teaspoon allspice

CRUST

1. No need to preheat the oven for the crust.
2. Set the mixer to low and combine the almonds, vanilla, artificial extract, artificial sweetener, and butter together. Beat until well blended.
3. Pour the crust into a 10-inch springform pan and press against the bottom only.
4. Bake for 10 minutes at 350 degrees Fahrenheit.
5. Remove the crust from the oven and set aside to cool.

FILLING

1. Preheat the oven to 300 degrees Fahrenheit.

2. Set the mixer to high and beat the cream cheese until fluffy with no lumps. Scrape down the sides of the bowl every 2 minutes.

3. Set the mixer to low and add pumpkin puree, artificial sweetener, vanilla, heavy whipping cream, eggs, almond flour, cinnamon, nutmeg, and allspice, mixing until it becomes smooth and creamy.

4. Pour the batter into the crust.

5. Bake the cheesecake for 2 hours.

6. Using a clean knife, check the center of the cheesecake by inserting the knife halfway through. If the knife comes out clean, then the cake is ready to be removed from the oven.

7. Leave the cheesecake on a cooling rack until you can see the sides coming away from the pan. Remove the cheesecake from the pan and place in the fridge for 4 hours before serving.

Chocolate Cheesecake

Makes 12 servings ♻ 4 ounces per serving ♻
4.2 net carbs per serving

CRUST

2 1/2 cups ground almonds
1/4 teaspoon vanilla extract
1/2 cup artificial sweetener
1/2 cup melted unsalted butter

FILLING

2 1/2 pounds softened cream cheese
1/2 cup sour cream
2 cups artificial sweetener
1 teaspoon vanilla extract
2 teaspoons lemon juice
1 1/2 cups heavy whipping cream
2 egg yolks
6 eggs
4 ounces (4 squares) unsweetened baking chocolate

CRUST

1. No need to preheat the oven for the crust.

2. Set the mixer to low and combine the almonds, vanilla, artificial sweetener, and melted butter together. Beat until well blended.

3. Pour the crust in a 10-inch springform pan and press against the bottom and the sides.

4. Bake for 10 minutes at 350 degrees Fahrenheit.

5. Remove the crust from the oven and set aside to cool.

FILLING

1. Preheat the oven to 300 degrees Fahrenheit.

2. Set the mixer to high and whip the cream cheese until fluffy with no lumps. Scrape down the sides of the bowl every 2 minutes.

3. Set the mixer to low and add the sour cream, artificial sweetener, vanilla, lemon juice, heavy whipping cream, egg yolks, and eggs. Beat until smooth and creamy.

4. Add the melted chocolate and beat until the batter becomes uniformly chocolate in color.

5. Pour the batter into the crust.

6. Bake the cheesecake for 1 1/2 hours to 2 hours.

7. Using a clean knife, check the center of the cheesecake by inserting the knife halfway through. If the knife comes out clean, then the cake is ready to be removed from the oven.

8. Leave the cheesecake on a cooling rack until you can see the sides coming away from the pan. Transfer the cake to a nonstick pan and then place in the fridge until served.

Chocolate Orange Cheesecake

Makes 12 servings ❧ 3 3/4 ounces per serving ❧
4.8 net carbs per serving

CRUST

2 1/2 cups ground almonds
1/4 teaspoon vanilla extract
1/4 cup artificial sweetener
1/2 cup melted unsalted butter

FILLING

2 1/2 pounds cream cheese
1/2 cup sour cream
2 1/2 cups artificial sweetener
1 teaspoon vanilla extract
1/4 cup orange extract
1/4 cup grated orange peel
1 1/2 cups heavy whipping cream
2 egg yolks
5 eggs
4 ounces (4 squares) unsweetened baking chocolate

CRUST

1. No need to preheat the oven for crust.
2. Set the mixer to low and combine the ground almonds, vanilla, artificial sweetener, and melted butter together. Beat until well blended.
3. Pour the crust into a 10-inch springform pan and press against the bottom and the sides.
4. Bake for 10 minutes at 350 degrees Fahrenheit.
5. Remove from the oven and set aside to cool.

FILLING

1. Preheat the oven to 200 degrees Fahrenheit.
2. Set the mixer to high and whip the cream cheese until fluffy with no lumps. Scrape down the sides of the bowl every 2 minutes.
3. Set the mixer to low and add the sour cream, artificial sweetener, vanilla, orange extract, orange peel, heavy whipping cream, egg yolks, and eggs. Beat until smooth and creamy.
4. Add the melted chocolate and beat until the batter becomes uniformly chocolate in color.
5. Pour the batter into the crust.
6. Bake the cheesecake for 1 1/2 hours to 2 hours.
7. Using a clean knife, check the center of the cheesecake by inserting the knife halfway through. If the knife comes out clean, then the cake is ready to be removed from the oven.
8. Leave the cheesecake on a cooling rack until you can see the sides coming away from the pan. Transfer the cake to a nonstick pan and then place in the fridge until served.

Caramel Pecan Cheesecake

Makes 12 servings ⌒ゝ 2 ounces per serving ⌒ゝ
3.9 net carbs per serving

1 pound softened cream cheese

1 cup sour cream

1/2 cup artificial sweetener

1 teaspoon vanilla extract

11/2 teaspoon lemon juice

11/2 cup heavy whipping cream

2 eggs

2 cups chopped pecans

1 cup sugar-free caramel sauce

1. Preheat the oven to 300 degrees Fahrenheit.

2. Set the mixer to high and beat the cream cheese until fluffy with no lumps. Scrape down the sides of the bowl every 2 minutes.

3. Set the mixer to low and add sour cream, artificial sweetener, vanilla, lemon juice, heavy whipping cream, eggs, and chopped pecans. Beat until smooth and creamy.

4. Pour the cheesecake batter into a 10-inch springform cake pan.

5. Pour the caramel sauce into the center of the batter. Using the end of a fork, swirl the sauce to make a windmill design.

6. Bake the cheesecake for 1 1/2 hours to 2 hours.

7. Using a clean knife, check the center of the cheesecake by inserting the knife halfway through the cake. If the knife comes out clean, then the cake is ready to be removed from the oven.

8. Leave the cheesecake on a cooling rack until you can see the sides coming away from the pan. Transfer the cake to a nonstick pan and then place in the fridge until served.

4

Pies and Tarts

Silk Peanut Butter Pie

Makes 10 servings   ⌒   3/4 ounce per serving   ⌒
5.0 net carbs per serving

CRUST

2 1/2 cups almond flour
1/4 cup artificial sweetener
1/4 teaspoon vanilla extract
1/2 cup melted unsalted butter

FILLING

2 cups heavy cream
1 teaspoon vanilla extract
2 cups sugar-free peanut butter
1 cup artificial sweetener

CRUST

1. No need to preheat the oven for the crust.
2. Set the mixer to low. In a medium bowl, combine the almond flour, artificial sweetener, vanilla, and butter together. Beat until well blended.
3. Pour the crust into an 8-inch glass pie dish and press evenly about on the bottom and the sides.
4. Bake for 5 to 8 minutes at 350 degrees Fahrenheit.
5. Remove from the oven and place in the fridge.

FILLING

1. Set the mixer on high and beat the heavy cream and artificial sweetener until peaks form. Set aside.

2. Set the mixer to medium and combine the peanut butter and vanilla extract together. Beat until smooth.

3. Fold in the heavy cream and mix until well blended.

4. Remove the pie crust from the fridge and scoop the filling into the crust.

5. Place the pie into the fridge for 3 hours before serving.

6. You can use ground pecans instead of almond flour for the crust.

7. Store in the fridge.

Pumpkin Pie Dessert Cups

Makes 6 servings ⌒ 1/2 ounce per serving ⌒
2.0 net carbs per serving

2 cups ricotta cheese
1/2 cup artificial sweetener
1/4 teaspoon vanilla extract
1 tablespoon pumpkin spice
1/2 tablespoon nutmeg
1 1/2 tablespoons cinnamon
3 cups sugar-free whipped topping

1. Set the mixer to low and combine the ricotta cheese, artificial sweetener, vanilla, pumpkin spice, and nutmeg together. Beat until well blended.

2. Scoop the mixture into 6 small dessert bowls, filling them about 1/2 full.

3. Sprinkle a layer of cinnamon and then scoop the remaining mixture into the bowls.

4. Place the bowls in the fridge for 1 to 2 hours.

5. Add the whipped topping just before serving.

6. If you want to make this like a pie, you can use the cheesecake crust recipe. (See page 40.) This will change the net carb count to 2.8.

Chocolate Crème Pie

Makes 8 servings 〰 1 1/2 ounces per serving 〰
4 net carbs per serving

CRUST

2 cups almond flour

1/2 cup melted unsalted butter

1/2 cup artificial sweetener

FILLING

8 ounces softened cream cheese

2 1/2 cups heavy cream

1/4 teaspoon vanilla extract

1 ounce box sugar-free
chocolate pudding mix

CRUST

1. Preheat the oven to 350 degrees Fahrenheit.

2. Set the mixer to low. In a medium bowl, combine the almond flour, artificial sweetener, and unsalted butter together. Beat until well blended.

3. Pour the crust into an 8-inch glass pie dish and press crust evenly on the bottom and the sides.

4. Bake for 5 to 8 minutes.

5. Remove from the oven and place in the fridge.

FILLING

1. Set the mixer to high and beat the cream cheese until smooth with no lumps.

2. Set the mixer to low and add 2 cups of the heavy cream. Beat until smooth and creamy.

3. Add the vanilla extract and pudding mix and beat until thick and smooth.

4. Turn off the mixer and slowly add the remaining 1/2 cup of the heavy cream.

5. Set the mixer to low and beat until well blended.

6. Remove the pie crust from the fridge and pour the filling to the top of the shell.

7. Place the pie in the fridge for 2 to 3 hours before serving.

Butterscotch Crème Pie

Makes 8 servings   3 ounces per serving
4 net carbs per serving

CRUST

    2 cups almond flour

    1/2 cup artificial sweetener

    1 teaspoon vanilla

    1/2 cup melted unsalted butter

FILLING

    8 ounces cream cheese

    2 1/2 cups heavy cream

    1/4 teaspoon vanilla extract

    1 ounce box sugar-free butterscotch
       pudding mix

CRUST

1. Preheat the oven to 350 degrees Fahrenheit.

2. Set the mixer to low and combine the almond flour, artificial sweetener, vanilla, and butter together. Beat until well blended.

3. Pour the crust into an 8-inch glass pie dish and spread evenly on the bottom and the sides.

4. Bake for 5 to 8 minutes.

5. Remove from the oven and place in the fridge.

FILLING

1. Set the mixer to high and beat cream cheese until smooth with no lumps.
2. Set the mixer to low speed and add 2 cups of the heavy cream. Beat until smooth and creamy.
3. Add the vanilla and the pudding mix and beat until thick and smooth.
4. Turn off the mixer, then slowly add the remaining 1/2 cup of the heavy cream.
5. Set the mixer to low and beat until well blended.
6. Remove the pie crust from the fridge and pour the filling to the top of the shell.
7. Place the pie in the fridge for 2 to 3 hours before serving.

Vanilla Crème Pie

Makes 8 servings   ⌒   1 3/4 ounces per serving   ⌒
4 net carbs per serving

CRUST

2 cups almond flour
1/2 cup artificial sweetener
1/2 cup melted unsalted butter

FILLING

8 ounces softened cream cheese
3 cups heavy cream
1/4 teaspoon vanilla extract
1 ounce box sugar-free vanilla pudding mix

CRUST

1. Preheat the oven to 350 degrees Fahrenheit.
2. Set the mixer to low and combine the almond flour, artificial sweetener, and butter together. Beat until well blended.
3. Pour the crust into an 8-inch glass pie dish and spread evenly on the bottom and the sides.
4. Bake for 5 to 8 minutes.
5. Remove from and place in the fridge.

FILLING

1. Set the mixer to high and beat the cream cheese until smooth with no lumps.
2. Set the mixer to low and add 2 cups of the heavy cream. Beat until smooth and creamy.
3. Add the vanilla and pudding mix and beat until thick and smooth.
4. Turn off the mixer and slowly add the remaining 1 cup of the heavy cream.
5. Set the mixer to low and beat until well blended.
6. Remove the crust from the fridge and pour the filling to the top of the shell.
7. Place the pie in the fridge for 2 to 3 hours before serving.

Berry Coconut Crème Pie

Makes 6 servings ⤳ 3 ounces per serving ⤳
5.0 net carbs per serving

- 1 can (15 ounces) coconut milk
- 1 cup artificial sweetener
- 1 teaspoon vanilla extract
- 2 1/2 teaspoons plain gelatin
- 1 cup half and half cream
- 1 cup fresh sliced strawberries
- 1 cup fresh blueberries
- 1/2 cup unsweetened coconut
- 3 cups sugar-free whipped topping

1. Set the mixer to low and beat the coconut milk, artificial sweetener, and vanilla for two minutes.

2. In a separate bowl, dissolve the gelatin in the half and half. Mix until well blended. Set aside.

3. Add the strawberries, blueberries, and unsweetened coconut to the coconut mixture and mix by hand until well blended.

4. Using a rubber spatula, slowly fold in the gelatin mixture. Mix until smooth.

5. Fill 6 small dessert bowls with the mixture. Place in the fridge for 4 to 5 hours until set.

6. Add the whipped topping before serving.

Strawberry Crème Pie

Makes 8 servings ⌒ 1 3/4 ounces per serving ⌒
4.5 net carbs per serving

CRUST

2 cups almond flour
1/2 cup artificial sweetener
1/2 cup melted unsalted butter

FILLING

8 ounces softened cream cheese
2 1/2 cups heavy cream
1/4 teaspoon vanilla extract
1 ounce box sugar-free vanilla pudding mix
2 cups fresh sliced strawberries

CRUST

1. Preheat the oven to 350 degrees Fahrenheit.
2. Set the mixer to low and combine the almond flour, artificial sweetener, and butter together. Beat until well blended.
3. Pour the crust into an 8-inch glass pie dish and press on the bottom and the sides of the pie dish.
4. Bake for 5 to 8 minutes.
5. Remove from the oven and place in the fridge.

FILLING

1. Set the mixer to high and beat the cream cheese until smooth with no lumps.
2. Set the mixer to low and add 2 cups of the heavy cream. Beat until smooth and creamy.
3. Add the vanilla and pudding mix and beat until thick and smooth.
4. Turn off the mixer and slowly add the remaining 1/2 cup of the heavy cream.
5. Set the mixer to low and beat until well blended.
6. Fold in the sliced strawberries.
7. Remove the crust from the fridge and pour the filling to the top of the shell.
8. Place the pie in the fridge for 2 to 3 hours before serving.

Custard Pecan Pie

Makes 8 servings ⌒ 2 ounces per serving ⌒
5.4 net carbs per serving

CRUST

  2 cups almond flour
  1/2 cup artificial sweetener
  1/2 cup melted unsalted butter

FILLING

  8 ounces softened cream cheese
  2 1/2 cups heavy cream
  1/2 cup artificial sweetener
  1/4 teaspoon vanilla extract
  1 ounce box sugar-free vanilla pudding mix
  2 cups chopped pecans

CRUST

1. Preheat the oven to 350 degrees Fahrenheit.
2. Set the mixer to low and combine the almond flour, artificial sweetener and butter together. Beat until well blended.
3. Pour the crust into an 8-inch nonstick pie pan and press the crust evenly on the bottom and the sides.
4. Bake for 5 to 8 minutes.
5. Remove from the oven and place in the fridge.

FILLING

1. Set the mixer to high and beat the cream cheese until smooth with no lumps.
2. Set the mixer to low and add 2 cups of the heavy whipping cream and artificial sweetener. Beat until smooth and creamy.
3. Add the pudding mix and beat until thick and smooth.
4. Turn off the mixer and slowly add the remaining 1/2 cup of the heavy cream.
5. Set the mixer to low and beat until well blended.
6. Using a rubber spatula, fold in the chopped pecans.
7. Remove the crust from the fridge and pour the filling to the top of the shell.
8. Place the pie in the fridge for 2 to 3 hours before serving.

Macadamia Vanilla Cheese Pie

Makes 12 servings ✎ 4 ounces per serving ✎

6.0 net carbs per serving

CRUST

2 1/2 cups ground macadamia nuts

1/4 teaspoon vanilla extract

1/4 cup artificial sweetener

1/2 cup melted unsalted butter

FILLING

2 1/2 pounds cream cheese

1/2 cup sour cream

1 1/2 cups artificial sweetener

1 1/2 cups chopped macadamia nuts

2 1/2 teaspoons vanilla extract

1 cup heavy cream

2 egg yolks

6 eggs

CRUST

1. Preheat the oven to 350 degrees Fahrenheit.

2. Set the mixer to low and combine the ground macadamia nuts, vanilla, artificial sweetener, and butter together. Beat until well blended.

3. Pour the crust into a 10-inch glass pie dish and press against the bottom and the sides.

4. Bake for 10 minutes.

5. Remove from the oven and set on the counter to cool.

FILLING

1. Preheat the oven to 300 degrees Fahrenheit.

2. Set the mixer to high and beat the cream cheese until fluffy with no lumps. Scrape down the sides of the bowl every 2 minutes.

3. Set the mixer to low and add the sour cream, artificial sweetener, macadamia nuts, vanilla, heavy cream, egg yolks, and eggs. Beat until smooth and creamy.

4. Pour the filling into the crust.

5. Bake the pie for 1 1/2 hours to 2 hours. Using a clean knife, check the center of the pie by inserting the knife halfway through. If the knife comes out clean, then the pie is ready to be removed from the oven.

6. Leave the pie on a cooling rack for 15 minutes before storing in the fridge.

Pumpkin Pecan Pie

Makes 8 servings ⤾ 3 1/4 ounces per serving ⤾
5.2 net carbs per serving

- **4 eggs**
- **1 can (15 ounces) pumpkin puree**
- **3 cups half and half cream**
- **1 1/2 cups artificial sweetener**
- **1 cup chopped pecans, plus additional for garnish (optional)**
- **1/2 teaspoon allspice**
- **1/4 teaspoon nutmeg**
- **1 1/4 teaspoons cinnamon**
- **3 teaspoons vanilla extract**
- **1/4 teaspoon salt**
- **1/2 cup sour cream**
- **3 cups sugar-free whipped topping**

1. Preheat the oven to 300 degrees Fahrenheit.
2. Set the mixer to low and combine the eggs, pumpkin, half and half, artificial sweetener, chopped pecans, allspice, nutmeg, cinnamon, vanilla, salt, and sour cream together. Beat until well blended.
3. Pour the mixture slowly into a 10-inch glass pie dish.
4. Bake for 50 minutes to 1 hour.
5. Remove the pie from the oven and place in the fridge overnight.
6. Garnish with the sugar-free whipped topping and chopped pecans before serving.
7. Store in the fridge.

Chocolate Pecan
le Torte

Makes 8 servings   3/4 ounce per serving
4.8 net carbs per serving

TORTE

4 large eggs

1 1/2 cups artificial sweetener

1 teaspoon of vanilla extract

1 1/4 tablespoons baking
powder

1 cup unsweetened cocoa
powder

2 tablespoons almond flour

2 cups chopped pecans

TOPPING

1 cup heavy whipping cream

1/2 cup artificial sweetener

1. Preheat the oven to 350 degrees Fahrenheit.
2. Set the mixer to medium and combine the eggs, artificial sweetener, and vanilla together. Beat until
smooth.
3. Add the baking powder, cocoa, almond flour, and
chopped pecans. Beat until well blended.
4. Pour the batter into a 10-inch nonstick cake pan.
5. Bake for 20 to 25 minutes.
6. Insert a knife into the torte to make sure that it's completely baked. The knife should come out clean.
7. Place the torte on a cooling rack for 5 minutes. Then
transfer the torte to a large serving plate and place
into the fridge for 1 hour.
8. Prepare the topping. Set the mixer to high and beat
the heavy whipping cream and artificial sweetener
until peaks form. Do not overmix.
9. Spread the topping on each slice before serving.
10. Store in the fridge.

Chocolate Torte

Makes 8 servings   3/4 ounces per serving
4.8 net carbs per serving

TORTE

  4 large eggs
  1 1/2 cups artificial sweetener
  1 teaspoon vanilla extract
  3 teaspoons baking powder
  1 cup unsweetened cocoa powder
  2 tablespoons almond flour

TOPPING

  1 cup heavy whipping cream
  1/2 cup artificial sweetener

1. Preheat the oven to 350 degrees Fahrenheit.
2. Set the mixer to medium and combine the eggs, artificial sweetener, and vanilla extract together. Beat until smooth.
3. Slowly add the baking powder, cocoa powder, and almond flour and beat until well blended.
4. Pour the batter into a 10 inch nonstick cake pan.
5. Bake for 20 to 25 minutes.
6. Insert a knife into the torte to make sure that it's completely baked. The knife should come out clean.
7. Place the torte on a cooling rack for 5 minutes then transfer the torte to a large serving plate and place in the fridge for 1 hour.
8. Set the mixer to high and beat the heavy whipping cream and artificial sweetener until peaks form. Do not overmix.
9. Garnish each slice with the topping before serving.
10. Store in the fridge.

Vanilla Praline Pecan Torte

Makes 8 servings ⤳ 1 1/2 ounces per serving ⤳
4.2 net carbs per
serving

2 ounces softened cream cheese
4 eggs
1 cup artificial sweetener
2 cups ground pecans
2 teaspoons vanilla extract
1/2 ounce sugar-free vanilla pudding mix
1 cup vanilla praline whey powder
2 tablespoons softened unsalted butter
1/4 teaspoon salt
1 ounce sour cream
2 1/2 teaspoons baking powder
1 cup sugar-free fudge topping
1/2 cup sliced strawberries

1. Preheat the oven to 350 degrees Fahrenheit.

2. Set the mixer to medium and combine the cream cheese, eggs, artificial sweetener, pecans, vanilla, pudding mix, vanilla praline whey powder, unsalted butter, salt, sour cream, and baking powder together. Beat until well blended.

3. Pour the batter into a nonstick 10-inch cake pan.

4. Bake for 15 to 18 minutes or until the knife comes out clean.

5. Garnish with the sugar-free fudge topping and sliced strawberries before serving.

6. Store in the fridge.

Eggnog Cheesecake Tart with Chocolate Crust

Makes 12 servings ⌒ 4 1/4 ounces per serving ⌒
5.7 net carbs per serving

CRUST

2 1/2 cups ground almonds
1/4 teaspoon vanilla extract
1 cup artificial sweetener
1/2 cup melted unsalted butter
2 ounces (2 squares) melted baking chocolate

FILLING

2 1/2 pounds cream cheese
1/2 cup sour cream
1 cup almond flour
1 1/4 cups artificial sweetener
2 teaspoons vanilla extract
1 1/2 teaspoon nutmeg
1 1/2 teaspoon rum extract
1 teaspoon cinnamon
1 cup heavy whipping cream
2 egg yolks
6 eggs

CRUST

1. Preheat the oven to 350 degrees Fahrenheit.
2. Set the mixer to low and combine the almonds, vanilla, artificial sweetener, melted chocolate, and butter together. Beat until well blended.
3. Pour the crust into a 10-inch glass pie dish and press against the bottom and the sides.
4. Bake for 10 minutes.
5. Remove from the oven and set aside to cool.

FILLING

1. Preheat the oven to 200 degrees Fahrenheit.
2. Set the mixer to high and beat the cream cheese until fluffy with no lumps. Scrape down the sides of the bowl every 2 minutes.
3. Set the mixer to low and add the sour cream, almond flour, artificial sweetener, vanilla, nutmeg, rum extract, cinnamon, heavy whipping cream, egg yolks, and eggs. Beat until smooth and creamy.
4. Pour the filling into crust.
5. Bake cheesecake for 1 1/2 hours to 2 hours.
6. Using a clean knife, check the center of the cheesecake by inserting the knife halfway through. If the knife comes out clean, then the cake is ready to be removed from the oven.
7. Leave the cheesecake on a cooling rack until you can see the sides coming away from the pan. Transfer the cake to a nonstick pan and then place in the fridge until served.

5

Custards, Flan, and Mousse

Tiramisù

Makes 12 servings ∽ 2 1/2 ounces per serving ∽
3.5 net carbs per serving

1 1/2 pounds mascarpone cheese
1 1/2 cups artificial sweetener
2 teaspoons vanilla extract
2 1/2 cups heavy cream
3/4 teaspoon plain gelatin
1/2 teaspoon hot water
1 8-inch pound cake, sliced (see page 24)
1 cup strong coffee
1/4 cup unsweetened cocoa powder

1. Set the mixer to medium and cream together the mascarpone cheese, artificial sweetener, and vanilla. Beat until smooth. Set aside.

2. Set the mixer to medium. In a separate bowl, beat 2 cups of the heavy cream until peaks form. Set aside.

3. In a separate bowl, dissolve the gelatin in the hot water. Pour 1 cup of the heavy cream mixture at a time into the gelatin mix and stir until well blended. This method is called tempering. If you pour the gelatin into the mix all at one time, the mix will form lumps and will not set correctly. Set aside.

4. Place the slices of pound cake on the bottom of a 10-inch nonstick glass bowl.

5. Soak the pound cake with the coffee evenly and let sit for 10 minutes.

6. Using a rubber spatula, fold the whipped cream into the mascarpone mixture. Mix until well blended.

7. Using a spatula, spread the combined mixture evenly on the pound cake. Then sprinkle the cocoa on top.

8. Place in the fridge for 4 to 6 hours before serving.

White Chocolate Mousse Trifle

Makes 6 servings   1 ounce per serving

5.4 net carbs per serving

- 1 ounce box sugar-free instant white chocolate pudding mix
- 1/4 teaspoon vanilla extract
- 1/4 cup artificial sweetener
- 1 1/2 teaspoons almond extract
- 2 1/4 cups heavy whipping cream
- 3 cups sliced strawberries
- 3 cups sugar-free raspberry puree

1. Set the mixer to medium and combine the pudding mix, vanilla, artificial sweetener, almond extract, and heavy whipping cream together. Beat until stiff.

2. Place 1 cup of of the strawberries on the bottom of a large serving bowl. Pour 1/3 of the mousse on top of the strawberries, and then pour 1 cup of the raspberry puree on top of the mousse.

3. Repeat step two 2 more times, then place the trifle in the fridge for 4 hours before serving.

4. You can mix blueberries and raspberries with the strawberries for variety.

Egg Custard

Makes 1 serving   ⌒   3 1/2 ounces per serving   ⌒
4 net carbs per serving

> 1 egg
> 1 egg yolk
> 1 cup half and half creamer
> 3/4 cup artificial sweetener
> 1 teaspoon vanilla extract
> 1/8 teaspoon cinnamon

1. Preheat the oven to 325 degrees Fahrenheit.
2. Set the mixer to low and combine the egg, egg yolk, and half and half creamer together. Beat until well blended.
3. Add the artificial sweetener and vanilla and beat until well blended.
4. Pour mixture into an 4-inch glass pie dish. Place the dish into another larger dish as a water bath. If you don't use a water bath, the dessert will soufflé. Sprinkle the cinnamon on top before baking.
5. Bake for 30 to 40 minutes.
6. Remove from the oven and let cool for 15 minutes before serving. Custard may be served hot or cold.
7. Store in the fridge.

Spanish Flan

Makes 6 servings 〰 4 ounces per serving 〰
3 net carbs per serving

6 eggs
1 1/2 cups heavy cream
1 teaspoon vanilla extract
1/2 cup artificial sweetener

1. Preheat the oven to 350 degrees Fahrenheit.
2. Whisk the eggs, heavy cream, 1 cup water, vanilla, and artificial sweetener together until well blended.
3. Place 6 small baking dessert cups into a large pan with half-filled with water. You must use a water bath to avoid the flan to soufflé.
4. Sprinkle a small amount of artificial sweetener onto the bottom of the bowls.
5. Pour the mixture into the bowls, filling them about 3/4 full.
6. Bake for 40 to 50 minutes.
7. Remove from the oven and place in the fridge for 1 hour before serving.

Chocolate Spanish Flan

Makes 6 servings ❧ 4 ounces per serving ❧
3 net carbs per serving

6 eggs
1 1/2 cups heavy cream
1/2 cup unsweetened cocoa powder
1 teaspoon vanilla extract
1/2 cup artificial sweetener

1. Preheat the oven to 350 degrees Fahrenheit.
2. In a large bowl, whisk the eggs, heavy cream, 1 cup water, cocoa powder, vanilla, and artificial sweetener together until well blended.
3. Place 6 small baking dessert cups into a large pan half-filled with water. You must use a water bath to avoid the flan to soufflé.
4. Sprinkle a small amount of artificial sweetener on the bottom of the bowls.
5. Pour the mixture into the bowls, filling them about 3/4 full.
6. Bake for 40 to 50 minutes.
7. Remove from the oven and place in the fridge for 1 hour before serving.

Banana Spanish Flan

Makes 6 servings ∾ 4 ounces per serving ∾
3 net carbs per serving

6 eggs
1 3/4 cups heavy cream
1/2 cup banana extract
1 teaspoon vanilla extract
3/4 cup artificial sweetener

1. Preheat the oven to 350 degrees Fahrenheit.
2. Whisk the eggs, heavy cream, 1 cup water, banana extract, cocoa powder, vanilla, and artificial sweetener together until well blended.
3. Place 6 baking dessert cups into a large pan half-full of water. You must use a water bath to avoid the flan to soufflé.
4. Sprinkle a small amount of artificial sweetener on the bottom of the bowls.
5. Pour the mixture into the bowls, filling them about 3/4 full.
6. Bake for 40 to 50 minutes.
7. Remove from the oven and place in the fridge for 1 hour before serving.

Lemon Crème Mousse

Makes 4 servings ✑ 4 ounces per serving ✑
3 net carbs per serving

  2 cups heavy whipping cream
  1 cup artificial sweetener
  1 ounce sugar-free lemon pudding mix
  1 teaspoon vanilla extract
  2 cups sugar-free whipped topping
  1 cup sliced strawberries

1. Set the mixer to medium and combine the heavy cream, artificial sweetener, pudding mix and vanilla together. Beat until peaks form on the side of the bowl. Do not overmix.

2. Scoop the mousse into 4 small dessert cups and place in the fridge for 2 to 4 hours to set.

3. Garnish with the whipped topping and sliced strawberries before serving.

Raspberry Crème Mousse

Makes 4 servings   1 1/2 ounces per serving
3 net carbs per serving

2 cups heavy cream
1/2 ounce sugar-free vanilla pudding mix
1 cup artificial sweetener
1 teaspoon vanilla extract
1 ounce box sugar-free raspberry gelatin mix
2 cups sugar-free whipped topping
1/2 cup fresh raspberries

1. Set the mixer to high and combine the heavy cream, pudding mix, artificial sweetener, and vanilla together. Beat until peaks form. Do not overmix.
2. Add the dry raspberry gelatin and mix by hand until well blended.
3. Scoop the mousse into 4 small dessert cups and place in the fridge for 2 to 4 hours to set.
4. Garnish with the whipped topping and a few fresh raspberries before serving.

Banana Mousse Supreme

Makes 4 servings ～ 1 1/4 ounces per serving ～
3 net carbs per serving

- 1 ounce sugar-free banana pudding mix
- 2 cups heavy cream
- 1 cup artificial sweetener
- 1 teaspoon vanilla extract
- 1 cup sugar-free whipped topping

1. Prepare the banana pudding by using the directions on the package.
2. Set the mixer to high and combine the heavy cream, artificial sweetener, and vanilla together. Beat until peaks form. Do not overmix.
3. Using a rubber spatula, fold the whipped cream into the pudding.
4. Scoop the mousse into 4 small desserts cups and place in the fridge for 2 to 4 hours to set.
5. Garnish with whipped topping before serving.

Almond Mousse

Makes 5 servings ꙮ 3/4 ounces per serving ꙮ
3.7 net carbs per serving

> 1 ounce sugar-free instant vanilla pudding mix
> 1/4 cup almond extract
> 1/4 teaspoon vanilla extract
> 1/4 cup artificial sweetener
> 2 1/4 cups heavy whipping cream
> 2 cups toasted sliced almonds

1. Set the mixer to medium and combine the pudding mix, almond extract, vanilla, artificial sweetener, and heavy whipping cream together. Beat until stiff.

2. Scoop into 5 small dessert bowls and garnish the top with toasted almonds.

3. Place the bowls in the fridge for 3 hours before serving.

Oreo Mousse

Makes 6 servings   3 ounces per serving
5.2 net carbs per serving

- **8 ounces softened cream cheese**
- **1 ounce sugar-free instant vanilla pudding mix**
- **1 teaspoon vanilla extract**
- **1/2 cup artificial sweetener**
- **2 1/4 cups heavy whipping cream**
- **16 Oreo cookies (remove the white crème in the center of 10 of the cookies)**

1. Set the mixer to medium and combine the cream cheese, pudding mix, vanilla, artificial sweetener, almond extract, and heavy whipping cream together. Beat until stiff.

2. Break up the 10 cookies without the cream filling and fold them into the mousse, using a rubber spatula.

3. Scoop the mousse into 6 small dessert bowls and garnish each bowl with the remaining 6 cookies.

4. Place the bowls in the fridge for 3 hours before serving.

Tapioca

Makes 8 servings ∽ 1 ounce per serving ∽
1.3 net carbs per serving

3 tablespoons tapioca
1 ounce sugar-free vanilla pudding mix (not instant)
2 1/2 cups half and half cream
1 cup artificial sweetener
4 egg whites
1/4 teaspoon vanilla extract
1 cup sugar-free whipped topping

1. Presoak the tapioca in 2 cups room-temperature water for 1 hour and drain. Set aside.

2. In a medium saucepan, on high heat, combine the pudding mix, half and half, 1 cup of water, artificial sweetener, tapioca, and vanilla together. Stir until the mixture comes to a boil, approximately 10 minutes. Set aside.

3. Set the mixer on high and beat the egg whites until peaks form. Do not overmix.

4. Using a rubber spatula, fold the egg whites into the hot tapioca.

5. Place in the fridge for 6 to 8 hours.

6. Garnish with the sugar-free whipped topping before serving.

White Chocolate Crème Mousse

Makes 5 servings   1 ounce per serving

4.2 net carbs per serving

1 ounce sugar-free instant white chocolate pudding mix
1/4 teaspoon vanilla extract
1/4 cup artificial sweetener
1 1/2 teaspoons almond extract
2 1/4 cups heavy whipping cream
1 cup sugar-free white chocolate shavings

1. Set the mixer to medium and combine the pudding mix, vanilla, artificial sweetener, almond extract, and heavy whipping cream together. Beat until stiff.

2. Pour mixture into 5 small dessert bowls and garnish with the white chocolate shavings.

3. Place the bowls into the fridge for 3 hours before serving.

4. Add the sliced strawberries on top as an added touch.

White Berry Cream Dessert

Makes 6 servings   2 ounces per serving

4.0 net carbs per serving

1 ounce sugar-free instant white chocolate pudding mix

1/4 teaspoon vanilla extract

8 ounces softened cream cheese

1 cup heavy whipping cream

1 cup seasonal berries (strawberries, blueberries, or raspberries)

2 cups unsweetened toasted coconut, at room temperature

1. Set the mixer to medium and combine the pudding mix, vanilla, cream cheese, 1 cup cold water, and heavy whipping cream together. Beat until smooth and creamy.

2. Scoop the mixture into 6 small desserts bowls, filling them halfway. Add the berries. Then scoop the remaining mixture into the bowls.

3. Garnish the top with more berries.

4. Sprinkle the toasted coconut on the edges of each bowl.

5. Place the bowls in the fridge for 2 to 3 hours before serving.

Eggnog Mousse

Makes 5 servings   1 3/4 ounces per serving

4.6 net carbs per serving

5 ounces of softened cream cheese

1 cup heavy whipping cream

1 ounce sugar-free instant vanilla pudding mix

1/4 cup artificial sweetener

1 1/4 teaspoon nutmeg

1/4 teaspoon ginger powder

1 1/4 teaspoon rum extract

1 teaspoon vanilla extract

1 teaspoon cinnamon

1. Set the mixer to medium and combine the cream cheese, heavy whipping cream, pudding mix, artificial sweetener, and 1 cup of cold water together. Beat until smooth and creamy.

2. Add the nutmeg, ginger, rum extract and vanilla and beat until well blended.

3. Scoop the mousse into 5 medium-size dessert bowls and chill in the fridge for 4 hours.

4. Sprinkle cinnamon on top before serving.

5. For a different taste, you can use sugar-free chocolate pudding mix.

Chocolate Cream Custard

Makes 2 servings   4 ounces per serving
1.0 net carbs per serving

    4 tablespoons softened unsalted butter
    4 ounces softened cream cheese
    1/2 cup unsweetened cocoa powder
    1/2 cup artificial sweetener
    2 egg yolks
    1/2 teaspoon vanilla extract
    1/2 cup heavy whipping cream
    2 cups sliced bananas

1. Using a double boiler, on low heat, melt together the butter, cream cheese, cocoa, artificial sweetener, egg yolks, vanilla, and the heavy whipping cream for 10 to 15 minutes, until completely smooth in texture. Do not boil.

2. Pour the custard into a serving bowl and place in the fridge for 4 hours.

3. Serve with sliced bananas.

4. For a different twist, use unsweetened white cocoa powder and add raspberries. The raspberries will add to the net carb total, increasing it to 1.6 per serving.

Bread Pudding

Makes 8 servings ⟶ 1 1/2 ounces per serving ⟶
3.0 net carbs per
serving

- 1 cup heavy cream
- 1/2 cup artificial sweetener
- 2 eggs
- 1/4 teaspoon salt
- 1/4 teaspoon vanilla extract
- 3 slices low carb bread (fresh)
- 1/4 cup unsalted butter
- 1/4 teaspoon cinnamon

1. Preheat the oven to 350 degrees Fahrenheit.
2. Set the mixer to low and combine the heavy cream, 1 cup of water, artificial sweetener, eggs, salt, and vanilla together. Beat until smooth. Set aside.
3. Cut the bread into 1/2 inch squares.
4. Spray the bottom of a deep casserole dish with a non-stick baking spray and place the bread evenly on the bottom.
5. Pour the cream mixture over the bread and dot with butter.
6. Sprinkle with the cinnamon.
7. Place the casserole dish into another larger dish and put 1 1/2 inches of hot water to make a water bath. Do not cover.
8. Bake for 30 to 40 minutes. Using a clean knife, check the center of the pudding by inserting a knife halfway through the pudding. If the knife comes out clean then the pudding is ready to be removed from the oven.
9. Store in the fridge until served.

Crème Brûlée

Makes 5 servings ◈ 3 ounces per serving ◈
4 net carbs per serving

8 egg yolks
1/2 cup artificial sweetener
2 1/2 cups heavy cream
1 teaspoon vanilla extract

1. Preheat the oven to 300 degrees Fahrenheit.

2. Set the mixer to low and combine the egg yolks and artificial sweetener together. Beat until it is completely incorporated into a paste.

3. Add the heavy cream and vanilla and beat until well blended.

4. Remove any large bubbles on top of the mix by tapping the sides of the bowl.

5. Place 5 medium-size dessert bowls into a large pan half-filled with water for a water bath.

6. Pour the mixture into the bowls, filling them about 3/4 full.

7. Bake for 50 to 60 minutes, or until the edges are separating from the sides of the bowls. When you lightly shake the bowls, there should not be any loose liquid. If you need to bake this dessert a little bit longer, do not increase the temperature. Just leave it in longer, 10 minutes at a time, checking by shaking the bowls until you no longer see liquid.

8. Remove the bowls from the water bath and place them in the fridge for 2 to 3 hours.

9. If you want to get the traditional crème brûlée affect, sprinkle artificial sweetener on top and burn with a torch or long lighter. Do not touch the hot sugar on top.

10. Store in the fridge until served.

6

Fudge, Chocolate, and Candy

Guilt-Free Fudge

Makes 12 servings ∽ 3/4 ounce per serving ∽
1 net carb per serving

4 ounces (4 squares) unsweetened baking chocolate
1 cup softened unsalted butter
1/2 teaspoon vanilla extract
1 cup artificial sweetener
1 cup heavy cream

1. On medium heat, using a wooden spoon, mix the chocolate, butter, vanilla, and artificial sweetener together. Stir until they come to a boil, approximately 10 to 15 minutes.

2. Remove from the heat and stir in the heavy cream until smooth.

3. Taste the mixture before pouring. If you need more sweetener this is the time to add slowly to taste.

4. Pour the mix into an 8-inch glass container and place in the fridge for 4 to 5 hours.

5. Remove from the fridge and cut into 2-inch squares.

6. Store in the fridge.

Nutty Peanut Butter Fudge

Makes 12 servings ∽ 3/4 ounce per serving ∽
3 net carbs per serving

- 1 1/2 cups heavy cream
- 5 ounces (5 squares) unsweetened baking chocolate
- 1 1/4 cups artificial sweetener
- 1/4 teaspoon vanilla extract
- 1/4 cup sugar-free peanut butter
- 1/2 cup chopped pecans
- 1 ounce sugar-free chocolate pudding mix

1. In a medium saucepan on low heat, using a wooden spoon, mix together the heavy cream, chocolate, peanut butter, and vanilla until melted, approximately 10 to 12 minutes.
2. Remove from heat and stir in the artificial sweetener.
3. Place the mixture in a bowl. Set the mixer to medium and beat until smooth.
4. Using a rubber spatula, fold the pecans and pudding mix into the mixture.
5. Pour the mixture into an 8-inch glass container and place in the fridge for 2 hours.
6. Remove from the fridge and cut into 2-inch squares.
7. Store in the fridge until served.

White Chocolate Fudge Dreams

Makes 6 serving ∼ 1/2 ounce per serving ∼
1 net carb per serving

2 ounces (2 squares) unsweetened baking chocolate
1/2 cup softened unsalted butter
2 tablespoons heavy cream
1 teaspoon vanilla extract
1 1/2 cups artificial sweetener

1. In a medium saucepan on low heat, using a wooden spoon, mix together the white chocolate and butter until melted, approximately 10 to 12 minutes.

2. Remove from the heat and slowly stir in the heavy cream, vanilla, and artificial sweetener.

3. Pour the mixture into an 8-inch glass container and place in the fridge for 2 hours.

4. Remove from the fridge and cut into 2-inch pieces.

5. Store in the fridge until served.

Little Boo's Brownies

Makes 10 servings ⟋⟍ 3/4 ounce per serving ⟋⟍
5.5 net carbs per serving

1 cup softened unsalted butter

1 cup unsweetened cocoa powder

2 cups artificial sweetener

1/4 teaspoon salt

2 teaspoons vanilla extract

4 eggs

1/2 cup almond flour

1/2 cup oat flour (if you can't find oat flour, double the quantity of almond flour)

1/2 cup chopped walnuts (optional)

1. Preheat the oven to 350 degrees Fahrenheit.
2. Set the mixer to low and combine the butter, cocoa powder, artificial sweetener, salt, and vanilla together. Beat until smooth and creamy.
3. Add the eggs, almond flour, and oat flour and beat for only 1 minute. Do not overmix.
4. If you plan to add walnuts, fold them into the batter now, using a rubber spatula.
5. Pour the batter into a nonstick full sheet pan.
6. Bake for 20 to 25 minutes.
7. Remove from the oven and allow to cool for 20 minutes before serving.
8. Store in a dry, airtight container.

Brownie Bites

Makes 8 servings   ⌘   1 ounce per serving   ⌘
2.5 net carbs per serving

2 cups softened salted butter
1/2 cup unsweetened cocoa powder
2 cups artificial sweetener
1/4 teaspoon vanilla extract
1/2 cup ground walnuts
4 eggs
2 cups sugar-free whipped topping

1. Preheat the oven to 375 degrees Fahrenheit.
2. Place the butter in a microwave bowl and microwave on low until melted. Do not overcook. Set aside.
3. Set the mixer to low and combine the butter, cocoa powder, artificial sweetener, vanilla, ground walnuts, and eggs together. Beat until smooth.
4. Pour the batter into a 8-inch nonstick cake pan slowly.
5. Bake for 25 to 30 minutes.
6. Remove the cake from the oven and allow to cool for 15 minutes.
7. Cut the brownies into small squares.
8. Serve with the whipped topping.
9. Store the brownies in a dry, airtight container.

Chocolate Meal Shake

Makes 1 serving ⌒ 12 ounces per serving ⌒
8 net carbs per serving

1/4 cup vanilla protein powder
1/4 cup heavy cream
1 ounce softened cream cheese
1 teaspoon vanilla extract
1/4 cup artificial sweetener
1 1/2 tablespoons unsweetened cocoa powder
7 ice cubes
1 tablespoon sugar-free peanut butter (optional)

1. Place all the ingredients into a blender and cover. Mix on low speed until the ice cubes are completely chopped.
2. Add 1/4 cup of water and mix on low speed until well blended.
3. If desired, add the peanut butter and mix until well blended. Add 4 more net carbs if the peanut butter is added.

Peanut Butter Cup Poppers

Makes 12 servings ∽ 1/2 ounce per serving ∽
1.5 net carbs per serving

1 cup softened unsalted butter
1 1/2 ounces (1 1/2 squares) unsweetened baking chocolate
3/4 cups artificial sweetener
1/4 teaspoon vanilla extract
2 1/2 tablespoons heavy cream
2 tablespoons smooth sugar-free peanut butter

1. Place the butter and chocolate in a microwave bowl. Microwave on low until completely melted, approximately 3 to 5 minutes, stirring every 60 seconds.
2. Remove and add the artificial sweetener, vanilla, and heavy cream. Using a wooden spoon, stir until completely smooth.
3. Pour the mixture into 12 mini nonstick muffin cups, filling them about 1/2 full.
4. Using a 1/4 teaspoon measuring spoon, drop a scoop of peanut butter on top of the chocolate mixture in each cup.
5. Fill the cups with the remaining chocolate mixture.
6. Freeze for 3 hours before serving.
7. Store in the freezer.

Chocolate Frozen Drops

Makes 12 servings ∽ 3/4 ounce serving ∽
3 net carbs per serving

- 1 1/2 cups heavy whipping cream
- 1/4 cup artificial sweetener
- 6 1/2 ounces softened cream cheese
- 1/4 teaspoon vanilla extract
- 1/2 cup half and half cream
- 1 ounce instant sugar-free chocolate pudding mix
- 1 ounce sugar-free peanut butter (optional)

1. Set the mixer to high and combine the heavy cream and artificial sweetener together. Beat until peaks form. Set aside.
2. Set the mixer to medium and combine the cream cheese, vanilla, and half and half together in a separate bowl. Beat until smooth.
3. Set the mixer to low and add the pudding mix slowly. Beat until smooth.
4. Using a rubber spatula, fold the chocolate mix into the heavy whipping cream.
5. Using a pastry bag with a large tip, squeeze drops about 1/2-inch size onto a piece of parchment paper.
6. Freeze for 4 to 6 hours before serving.
7. You can add sugar-free peanut butter to the mixture for an extra kick. Add an additional 4 net carbs if using peanut butter.
8. Store in the freezer.

Cream Cheese
Chocolate Squares

Makes 8 servings   3/4 ounce per serving
2.7 net carbs per serving

1/4 cup unsalted butter
1 ounces (1 squares) unsweetened baking chocolate
1 teaspoon vanilla extract
4 ounces cream cheese
1 cup artificial sweetener
1/4 cup heavy cream
1/4 tablespoon unsweetened cocoa powder

1. In a medium saucepan on medium heat using a wooden spoon, combine the butter, chocolate, vanilla, cream cheese, artificial sweetener, heavy cream, and cocoa powder together. Stir until smooth, approximately 8 to 10 minutes.

2. Remove from the heat and stir in the heavy cream.

3. Pour into an 8-inch glass container and place in the fridge 4 to 5 hours.

4. Remove from the fridge and cut into 1/2 inch pieces.

5. Store in the fridge until served.

Peanut Butter Squares

Makes 8 servings   3/4 ounce per serving
2.5 net carbs per serving

    1/4 cup softened unsalted butter
    1 ounces (1 squares) unsweetened baking chocolate
    1 teaspoon vanilla extract
    4 ounces softened cream cheese
    1 cup artificial sweetener
    4 tablespoons sugar-free peanut butter
    1/4 cup heavy cream

1. In a medium saucepan on medium heat using a wooden spoon, combine the butter, chocolate, vanilla, cream cheese, artificial sweetener, and peanut butter together. Stir until smooth, approximately 10 minutes. Use smooth peanut butter for a creamier texture.

2. Remove from the heat and stir in heavy cream.

3. Pour into an 8-inch glass container and place in the fridge for 4 to 5 hours.

4. Remove from the fridge and cut into 1/2 inch pieces.

5. Place in the fridge until served.

Chocolate Raspberry Truffles

Makes 8 servings ⌒ 2 ounces per serving ⌒
1 net carb per serving

1 cup heavy cream
1 cup unsweetened cocoa powder
1/2 cup softened unsalted butter
1/4 teaspoon vanilla extract
3/4 cup artificial sweetener
1/2 cup sugar-free raspberry preserves

1. In a medium saucepan on low heat, use a wooden spoon to combine the heavy cream, cocoa, butter, and vanilla together. Stir until smooth, approximately 8 to 10 minutes.

2. Remove from the heat and add artificial sweetener. Stir until smooth.

3. Pour the chocolate mixture into a glass container and place in the fridge for 30 minutes.

4. Using a 1/2 ounce scoop or a tablespoon, shape the mixture into 8 balls.

5. With a pastry bag and a small tube tip, squeeze the raspberry preserves into each ball. Do not squeeze hard or the filling will come out of the other end of the truffle. You can use any flavor sugar-free preserve that you desire.

6. You may roll the truffles in unsweetened cocoa powder to give them a velvet look. This will not add to the net carb total.

7. Place the truffles in the fridge for 1 hour before serving.

Hazelnut Truffle Bites

Makes 14 servings ⌒ 1/2 ounce per serving ⌒
2.4 net carbs per serving

2 tablespoons sugar-free peanut butter
1 tablespoon unsweetened cocoa powder
1/4 cup heavy whipping cream
2 teaspoons hazelnut syrup
3/4 cup artificial sweetener
1 1/2 cups unsweetened coconut

1. Set the mixer to medium and combine the peanut butter, cocoa, heavy whipping cream, hazelnut syrup, and artificial sweetener together. Beat until smooth.

2. Place a large piece of wax paper onto a table and sprinkle the coconut onto the wax paper.

3. Using a 1/2 ounce scoop or a tablespoon, shape the mixture into 14 balls.

4. Roll the balls in the coconut until completely covered.

5. Place the truffles into the fridge for 1 hour before serving.

Cocoa Peanut Butter Truffles

Makes 8 servings ⌒ 1/2 ounce per serving ⌒
2 net carbs per serving

> 4 tablespoons sugar-free peanut butter
> 1 tablespoon unsweetened cocoa powder
> 1/4 cup heavy whipping cream
> 3/4 cup artificial sweetener
> 1 1/2 cups unsweetened coconut

1. Set the mixer to medium and combine the peanut butter, cocoa, heavy whipping cream and artificial sweetener together. Beat until smooth.
2. Place a large piece of wax paper onto a table and sprinkle the coconut onto the wax paper.
3. Using a 1/2 ounce scoop or a tablespoon, shape the mixture into 8 balls.
4. Rolls the balls in the coconut until completely covered.
5. Place the truffles into the fridge for 1 hour before serving.
6. You can roll the truffles in unsweetened cocoa powder or chopped almonds as well. Chopped almonds will add to the net carb total, increasing it to 2.6.

Mint Chocolate Delights

Makes 6 servings ⌒ 3/4 ounce per serving ⌒
1 net carb per serving

2 ounces (2 squares) unsweetened baking chocolate
1/2 cup softened unsalted butter
2 tablespoons heavy cream
1 teaspoon vanilla extract
1 cup artificial sweetener
1/2 teaspoon mint extract

1. In a medium saucepan on low heat, using a wooden spoon, combine the chocolate and butter together. Stir until smooth, approximately 6 to 8 minutes.

2. Remove from the heat and slowly add the heavy cream, vanilla, artificial sweetener, and mint extract. Stir until well blended. Do not overpour the mint extract. It is very strong and can burn your mouth.

3. Pour the mixture into an 8-inch glass container and place in the fridge for 2 hours.

4. Remove from the fridge and cut into 2-inch pieces.

5. Store in the fridge until served.

Peanut Butter Delights

Makes 6 servings   3/4 ounce per serving   1 net carb per serving

> **2 ounces (2 squares) unsweetened baking chocolate**
> **1/2 cup softened unsalted butter**
> **2 tablespoons heavy cream**
> **1 teaspoon vanilla extract**
> **1 1/2 cups artificial sweetener**
> **1/2 cup sugar-free peanut butter**

1. In a medium saucepan on low heat, using a wooden spoon, combine the chocolate and butter together. Stir until smooth, approximately 8 to 10 minutes.

2. Remove from the heat and slowly add the heavy cream, vanilla, artificial sweetener, and peanut butter. Stir until well blended. You can use either creamy or crunchy peanut butter.

3. Pour the mixture into an 8-inch glass container and place in the fridge for 2 hours.

4. Remove from the fridge and cut into 2-inch pieces.

5. Store in the fridge until served.

Cherry Squares

Makes 8 servings ✐ 1/2 ounce per serving ✐
1 net carb per serving

2 ounces (2 squares) unsweetened baking chocolate
1/2 cup softened unsalted butter
2 tablespoons heavy cream
1 teaspoon vanilla extract
1 1/2 cups artificial sweetener
1 tablespoon cherry extract

1. In a medium saucepan on low heat, using a wooden spoon, combine the bakers chocolate and unsalted butter together. Stir until smooth, approximately 7 minutes.

2. Remove from the heat and slowly add the heavy cream, vanilla, artificial sweetener, and cherry extract. Stir until well blended. Do not overpour the cherry extract.

3. Pour the mixture into an 8-inch glass container and place in the fridge for 2 hours.

4. Remove from the fridge and cut into 2-inch pieces.

5. Store in the fridge until served.

Macadamia Nut Chocolate Melt-A-Ways

Makes 8 servings   ⤳   1/2 ounce per serving   ⤳
3.2 net carbs per serving

> 2 ounces (2 squares) unsweetened baking chocolate
> 3/4 cup softened unsalted butter
> 1/2 cup heavy cream
> 1 teaspoon vanilla extract
> 1 3/4 cups artificial sweetener
> 1 cup finely chopped macadamia nuts

1. In a medium saucepan on low heat, using a wooden spoon, combine the chocolate and butter together. Stir until smooth, approximately 7 minutes.

2. Remove from the heat and slowly add the heavy cream, vanilla, artificial sweetener, and macadamia nuts. Stir until well blended.

3. Pour the mixture into an 8-inch glass container and place in the fridge for 2 hours.

4. Remove from the fridge and cut into 2-inch pieces.

5. Store in the fridge until served.

Cappuccino Hazelnut Candy

Makes 5 servings ～ 1/2 ounce per serving ～
3 net carbs per serving

- 1/4 cup instant coffee
- 1 tablespoon unsweetened cocoa powder
- 1/4 cup heavy whipping cream
- 1 cup artificial sweetener
- 1/2 teaspoon vanilla extract
- 1 cup ground hazelnuts

1. Set the mixer to medium, and combine the instant coffee, cocoa, heavy whipping cream, artificial sweetener, vanilla, and ground hazelnuts together. Beat until smooth.
2. Place a large piece of wax paper onto a table and scoop the batter onto the paper. Fold the wax paper over the batter and roll the paper until it forms a log.
3. Place in the fridge for 3 hours or until hard.
4. Remove from the fridge and unwrap the candy.
5. Using a sharp knife, cut the candy log into 1/4-inch pieces.
6. Store in the fridge until served.

Chocolate Doughnut Fritters

Makes 20 servings ✑ 3/4 ounce per serving ✑
2.6 net carbs per serving

 1 quart cooking oil (corn, vegetable, or any light-flavored oil)
 3/4 cup melted unsalted butter
 1 1/2 tablespoons unsweetened cocoa powder
 1/2 cup artificial sweetener
 2 1/4 teaspoons baking powder
 1 egg
 3/4 cup almond flour
 1/2 teaspoon vanilla extract
 1/4 teaspoon cinnamon

1. Preheat the oil for frying the fritters in a large electric frying pan, set at 350 degrees Fahrenheit.

2. Set the mixer to low and combine the butter, cocoa, artificial sweetener, baking powder, egg, almond flour, vanilla, and cinnamon together. Beat until smooth and creamy.

3. Using a teaspoon, drop a small ball of batter into the oil. When the fritter starts to float, the oil is ready.

4. Fry the fritters for 1 minute on one side, then turn over and fry the other side for 45 seconds.

5. Using a metal spatula, remove the fritters and place them on a paper towel to drain.

6. While still warm, you can roll the fritters in artificial sweetener or cinnamon for flavoring.

Coconut Peanut Butter Truffles

Makes 10 servings ✑ 2 ounces per serving ✑
2 net carbs per serving

4 tablespoons sugar-free peanut butter
1 tablespoon unsweetened cocoa powder
1/4 cup heavy whipping cream
3/4 cup artificial sweetener
1 1/2 cups unsweetened coconut

1. Set the mixer to medium and combine the peanut butter, cocoa powder, heavy whipping cream and artificial sweetener together. Beat until smooth.
2. Place a large piece of wax paper onto a table and sprinkle the coconut on the wax paper.
3. Using a 1/2 ounce scoop or a tablespoon, shape the mixture into 10 balls. Roll each ball in the coconut until completely covered.
4. Place the truffles in the fridge for 1 hour before serving.
5. You can also roll the truffles in unsweetened cocoa powder or chopped almonds. Almonds will add 1.1 net carbs per serving, increasing the total to 3.1 net carbs.

Chocolate Coconut Crunch Cups

Makes 12 servings ✺ 1/2 ounce per serving ✺
1.3 net carbs per serving

3 ounces (3 squares) unsweetened baking chocolate
4 tablespoons softened unsalted butter
1/4 cup heavy whipping cream
1/4 teaspoon vanilla extract
1/4 teaspoon coconut extract
1/4 teaspoon almond extract
1 cup of artificial sweetener
3 tablespoons unsweetened coconut

1. Line a mini muffin pan with foil cups.

2. In a double boiler on low heat, using a wooden spoon, combine the chocolate and butter together. Stir until smooth, approximately 15 minutes.

3. With the heat still on, add the heavy whipping cream, vanilla, coconut extract, almond extract, artificial sweetener, and coconut and stir until well blended.

4. Remove the mixture from the heat and pour into the foil cups, filling them about 3/4 full.

5. Place the pan in the freezer for 8 hours or until the mixture become hard.

6. Remove from the freezer and serve.

7. For Peanut Butter Crunches, add 2 tablespoons of sugar-free crunchy peanut butter to the mixture. Your net carb count will increase to 5.3 per serving when adding peanut butter.

Chocolate Joles

Makes 10 servings ∿ 1 1/2 ounces per serving ∿
5.1 net carbs per serving

8 ounces softened cream cheese
1/4 cup half and half cream
1 tablespoon softened unsalted butter
3 ounces (3 squares) unsweetened baking chocolate
1 teaspoon vanilla extract
1 cup unsweetened cocoa powder
1 cup artificial sweetener

1. In a large saucepan on low heat, using a wooden spoon, combine the cream cheese, half and half, butter, chocolate, and vanilla together. Stir until smooth, approximately 12 to 15 minutes.

2. Using a rubber spatula, fold the cocoa and artificial sweetener into the mixture and mix until well blended.

3. Using a 1/2 scoop or a tablespoon, shape the mixture into 10 balls and place on a piece of wax paper.

4. Place the balls in the fridge for 3 hours.

5. Store in the fridge until served.

7

Ice Cream
and
Frozen
Treats

Simple Vanilla Ice Cream

Makes 1 serving ⌒ 4 ounces per serving ⌒
3.2 net carbs per serving

2 eggs
1/2 cup artificial sweetener
1 teaspoon vanilla extract
2 cups heavy cream
1 electric ice cream maker

1. In a medium bowl, using a wooden spoon, combine the eggs and artificial sweetener together. Stir until thick and smooth.
2. Add the vanilla and heavy cream and stir for 30 seconds.
3. Do not cut back on the quantity of heavy cream, or the mixture will not freeze correctly.
4. Pour the mixture into an ice cream maker and follow the ice cream directions on the machine.
5. Store in the freezer until served.

Strawberry Ice Cream

Makes 1 serving ↝ 4 ounces per serving ↝
3.8 net carbs per serving

2 eggs
1/2 cup artificial sweetener
1 teaspoon vanilla extract
1 1/2 cups heavy cream
1/2 cup sliced strawberries, lightly crushed
1 electric ice cream maker

1. In a medium bowl, using a wooden spoon, combine the eggs and artificial sweetener together. Stir until thick and smooth.

2. Add the vanilla and heavy cream, and stir to blend well.

3. Do not cut back on the quantity of heavy cream, or the mixture will not freeze correctly.

4. Add the strawberries and stir for 30 seconds.

5. Pour the mixture into an ice cream maker and follow the ice cream directions on the machine.

6. Store in the freezer until served.

Blueberry Ice Cream

Makes 1 serving ∽ 5.3 ounces per serving ∽
3.7 net carbs per serving

2 eggs
1/2 cup artificial sweetener
1 teaspoon vanilla extract
1 1/2 cups heavy cream
1/2 cup whole blueberries, lightly crushed
1 electric ice cream maker

1. In a medium bowl, using a wooden spoon, combine the eggs and artificial sweetener together. Stir until thick and smooth.

2. Add the vanilla and heavy cream and stir to blend well.

3. Do not cut back on the quantity of heavy cream, or the mixture will not freeze correctly.

4. Add the blueberries and stir for 30 seconds.

5. Pour the mixture into an ice cream maker and follow the ice cream directions on the machine.

6. Store in the freezer until served.

Cinnamon Ice Cream

Makes 1 serving ❧ 4 ounces per serving ❧
3.0 carbs per serving

2 eggs
1 cup artificial sweetener
1 teaspoon vanilla extract
1 1/2 cups heavy cream
1/4 cup ground cinnamon
1 electric ice cream maker

1. In a medium bowl, using a wooden spoon, combine the eggs and artificial sweetener together. Stir until thick and smooth.

2. Add the vanilla, heavy cream, and ground cinnamon, and stir for 30 seconds.

3. Do not cut back on the quantity of heavy cream, or the mixture will not freeze correctly.

4. Pour the mixture into an ice cream maker and follow the ice cream directions on the machine.

5. Store in the freezer until served.

Chocolate Ice Cream

Makes 1 serving ~ 4 ounces per serving ~
2.8 net carbs per serving

2 eggs
1 1/2 cup artificial sweetener
1 teaspoon vanilla extract
1 1/2 cups heavy cream
1/2 cup unsweetened cocoa powder
1/4 cup sugar-free chocolate syrup
1 electric ice cream maker

1. In a medium bowl, using a wooden spoon, combine the eggs and artificial sweetener together. Stir until thick and smooth.

2. Add the vanilla, heavy cream, and chocolate syrup and stir to blend well.

3. Do not cut back on the quantity of heavy cream, or the mixture will not freeze correctly.

4. Sprinkle the cocoa over the surface of the mixture and stir for 30 seconds.

5. Pour the mixture into an ice cream maker and follow the ice cream directions on the machine.

6. Store in the freezer until served.

Peanut Butter Ice Cream

Makes 1 serving ❧ 5 ounces per serving ❧
3.6 net carbs serving

2 eggs
1 cup artificial sweetener
1 teaspoon vanilla extract
1 1/2 cups heavy cream
1 1/2 cups sugar-free peanut butter
1 electric ice cream maker

1. In a medium bowl, using a wooden spoon, combine the eggs and artificial sweetener together. Stir until thick and smooth.

2. Add the vanilla, peanut butter, and heavy cream and stir until well blended.

3. Do not cut back on the quantity of heavy cream, or the mixture will not freeze correctly.

4. Pour the mixture into an ice cream maker and follow the ice cream directions on the machine.

5. Store in the freezer until served.

Banana Ice Cream

Makes 1 serving ∽ 4 ounces per serving ∽
3.0 net carbs per serving

2 eggs
1 cup artificial sweetener
1 teaspoon vanilla extract
1 1/2 cups heavy cream
1/4 cup banana puree

1. In a medium bowl, using a wooden spoon, combine the eggs and artificial sweetener together. Stir until thick and smooth.
2. Add the vanilla and heavy cream and stir until well blended.
3. Do not cut back on the quantity of heavy cream, or the mixture will not freeze correctly.
4. Add the banana puree and stir for 30 seconds.
5. Pour the mixture into an ice cream maker and follow the ice cream directions on the machine.
6. Store in the freezer until served.

Frozen Chocolatesicles

Makes 10 servings ∾ 3/4 ounce servings ∾
2 net carbs per serving

> 1 ounce sugar-free instant chocolate pudding mix
> 1/2 cup artificial sweetener
> 2 cups heavy whipping cream

1. Setting the mixer to high, combine the pudding mix, artificial sweetener, and heavy whipping cream together. Beat until stiff.
2. Pour the mixture into 10 small dessert bowls.
3. Place the bowls in the freezer for 6 to 8 hours or until completely frozen.
4. Store in the freezer until served.

Toppings and Frostings

Chocolate Topping

Makes 4 servings ∿ 1/2 ounce per serving ∿
3 net carbs per serving

- **1 cup unsweetened cocoa powder**
- **1 cup hot water**
- **1 teaspoon vanilla extract**
- **1 cup artificial sweetener**

1. In a medium saucepan over high heat, using a wooden spoon, combine the cocoa, hot water, artificial sweetener, and vanilla together. Stir the mixture until it comes to a boil, approximately 12 to 15 minutes.

2. Remove from the heat and continue stirring for 1 more minute. If the mixture looks too thick, add a little bit more hot water and keep stirring until creamy.

3. Store in an airtight container in the fridge until served.

4. You may also microwave the topping for 1 minute before serving.

Vanilla Frosting for Cakes or Cupcakes

Frosts one 8-inch cake ➣ 4 1/4 ounces per serving ➣
1.0 net carbs per serving

1 1/2 cups artificial sweetener
3 egg whites at room temperature
1 teaspoon vanilla extract
1 teaspoon cream of tartar

1. In a double boiler on medium heat, using a whisk,
   combine the artificial sweetener, egg whites, vanilla,
   water and cream of tartar together. Stir until simmering, approximately 15 minutes.
2. Beat the simmering mixture with a hand mixer set on
   high until peaks form or until smooth, approximately 5
   minutes.
3. Remove from the heat and let cool.
4. Store in an airtight container in the fridge.

Chocolate Frosting
for Cakes or Cupcakes

Frosts one 8-inch cake ∽ 5 ounces per serving ∽
1.0 net carbs

　　2 cups artificial sweetener
　　3 egg whites at room temperature
　　1 teaspoon vanilla extract
　　1 teaspoon cream of tartar
　　1/2 cup unsweetened cocoa powder

1. In a double boiler on medium heat, using a whisk, combine the artificial sweetener, egg whites, vanilla, water, and cream of tartar together. Stir until simmering, approximately 15 minutes.

2. Beat the simmering mixture with a hand mixer set on high until peaks form or until smooth, approximately 5 minutes.

3. Using a rubber spatula, fold the cocoa into the mixture and mix until well blended.

4. Remove from the heat and let cool.

5. Store in an airtight container in the fridge.

Dipping Chocolate

Makes 30 servings ✐ 1 tablespoon per serving ✐
1 net carb per serving

1 cup cold coffee
1/2 cup artificial sweetener
3 1/2 tablespoons unsweetened cocoa powder
2 1/4 teaspoons cornstarch
1 teaspoon vanilla extract
1/2 teaspoon unsalted softened butter

1. In a small saucepan over medium heat, using a wooden spoon, combine the coffee, artificial sweetener, cocoa, and cornstarch together. Stir until smooth and thick, approximately 10 minutes.

2. Add the vanilla and butter and stir until well blended.

3. Remove from the heat and allow the chocolate to cool for several minutes before serving. This cooling stage will allow the chocolate to adhere to the fruit or food products being dipped.

4. You can substitute unsweetened chocolate syrup for the coffee. Add 1/2 additional artificial sweetener if you choose to do this. This will increase the net carbs to 1.5 per serving.

Glossary

Almonds: The kernels of the fruit of the almond tree. There are two types of almonds: sweet and bitter.

Bake: To cook in an oven with dry heat. The oven should always be heated for 10 to 15 minutes before baking.

Baking Powder: Leavening agent typically found as a double-acting baking powder, because it firstly reacts with liquids and secondly reacts with heat during baking. A good substitute for 1 teaspoon of baking powder is 1/4 teaspoon baking soda plus 1/2 teaspoon cream of tartar.

Baking Soda: Leavening agent activated by interacting with an acidic agent. Liquid ingredients such as sour milk, sour cream, buttermilk, yogurt, molasses, and lemon juice help baking soda produce the gases that make a batter rise. The batter must be baked as soon as possible after the liquid has interacted with the baking soda to produce the desired results.

Baking Sheet: A sheet of metal that is rigid and is used for baking cookies, breads, biscuits, etc. It usually has one or more edges that are turned up for ease in removing from the oven. Types include shiny, heavy-gauge aluminum, the standard used in most test kitchens for even baking and browning. Darkened, heavy-gauge pans will produce especially crisp exterior crusts desired for specialty baked goods. Insulated baking sheets are two sheets of aluminum with air space between.

Batter: A mixture of flour, liquid and other ingredients that is thin enough to pour.

Beat: To mix rapidly, smoothing the ingredients and adding air, using a wire whisk, electric hand mixer, or stand mixer.

Beating: Process of mixing food to introduce air and make it lighter or fluffier. Tools utilized to beat an ingredient or mixture, include a wooden spoon, hand whisk, or electric mixer.

Bitter Almonds: Since these are bitter, they are usually distilled into an essence or extract that is used in baking. The sale of bitter almonds is illegal in the United States.

Blend: Preparation method that combines ingredients with a spoon, beater, or liquefier to achieve a uniform mixture.

Boil: To cook submerged in a boiling liquid.

Boiling: Preparation method that cooks a liquid at a temperature of 212 degrees Fahrenheit degrees (100 degrees Celsius). To get it, boil fresh cold tap water, and then use it; boiled water is not hot tap water. A full rolling boil—a boil that cannot be stirred down with a spoon.

Cakes: Cakes are made from various combinations of refined flour, some form of shortening, sweetening, eggs, milk, leavening agent, and flavoring.

Cappuccino: Espresso coffee and scalded milk.

Carbohydrates: Carbohydrates are a group of organic compounds that contain carbon in combination with the same proportion of hydrogen and oxygen (as in water). All starches and sugars are carbohydrates. The body receives a large amount of heat and energy from carbohydrate foods. The body changes all carbohydrates into simple sugar and the surplus is stored in the body as fat (and in the liver as glycogen). A large excess of sugar is normally eliminated by the kidneys. The usual "sweet tooth" of people is the result of body hunger for carbohydrates. Children require more carbohydrates than adults because they must satisfy the needs of growing bodies.

Chilling: Process of cooling prepared or partially prepared food, without freezing it, in a refrigerator or on cracked ice.

Chop: To cut food into irregular pieces. The size is specified if it is critical to the outcome of the recipe.

Cocoa Powder: The dry powder that remains after cocoa butter is pressed out of chocolate liquor. The residue of fibrous and other solid materials containing the flavoring and coloring components of chocolate liquor after some or most of the fat has been removed with a hydraulic press.

Combine: To incorporate two or more ingredients together.

Cooking Spray: Aerosol cans sold in grocery stores containing vegetable or olive oil that can be sprayed in a fine mist. This spray is used for "oiling" cooking pans so food does not stick.

Cooling Rack: A rectangular grid of thick wire with "feet" that raise it above the countertop. It is used to cool cakes, cookies, and other baked goods when they come out of the oven. Products are cooled while in their pan for a short time and after the product is removed from the pan prior to storing or freezing.

Cream: To work one or more foods until smooth and creamy with a spoon or spatula, rubbing the food against the sides of the mixing bowl until of the consistency of cream.

Creaming: It is the process of beating room-temperature fat, usually butter and/or shortening, and crystalline sugar together to blend them uniformly and to incorporate air. This is done with an electric hand mixer or stand mixer. Creaming stops when the mixture is light and fluffy. The entrapped air that results is dispersed throughout the dough when the creamed mixture is combined with the other ingredients. This facilitates the even distribution of leavening gases and water vapor released during baking. This results in an increase in volume and fine, even crumb structure in the finished recipe.

Cream of Tartar: Common name for potassium bitartare, a by-product of wine-making. It's a major ingredient in baking powder and is used to stabilize beaten egg whites

Crème Brûlée: A rich custard with a brittle top crust of caramelized sugar. The French name means "burned cream "

Custard: Custard is a combination of eggs and milk, which may be sweetened or unsweetened, cooked in a double boiler (as soft custard), or baked (which gives it a jellylike consistency). Custards require slow cooking and gentle heat to prevent separation (curdling).

Cut: To divide food material with knife or scissors.

Cut and fold: A combination of two motions—to cut vertically through mixture and to turn over by sliding tool across bottom of mixing bowl at each turn. Proper folding prevents loss of air.

Deep-Fry: Hot fat or oil that is deep enough to cover food during frying.

Deep-Frying: Method of frying food by immersing it in hot fat or oil.

Dessert: Meaning a usually sweet food served as the final course of a meal. The word was first recorded in 1600 and it derives from a French word meaning "to clear the table." This etymology is still reflected in current table service, where it is customary to remove everything from the table that's not being used (salt/pepper shakers, breadbaskets, sometimes even flowers) before serving dessert.

Dissolve: Stirring a dry substance into a liquid until solids are no longer remaining. (For example: stirring sugar into water, yeast into water, etc.)

Double Boiler: Cooking utensil much like a bain-marie. Method of cooking without using direct heat; double boilers are used to warm or cook heat-sensitive food such as custards, delicate sauces, and chocolate. A double-pan arrangement whereby two pots are formed to fit together, with one sitting partway inside the other. A single lid fits both pans. The lower pot is used to hold simmering water, which gently heats the mixture in the upper pot. The saucepans can be made from stainless steel.

Dry Ingredients: Refers to the ingredients in a recipe, such as flours, sugar, leavening, salt, baking cocoa, spices, or herbs that may be blended before adding to another mixture in the recipe.

Dusting: Finishing method whereby flour, sugar, spice, or seasoning is lightly sprinkled over the top of the food item.

Eggs: The ova of chickens. In home baking, neither the shell color nor the grade of egg matter. The size standard recipes call for is large unless stated otherwise. Eggs perform many functions—leavening, binding, thickening, coating, or glazing, emulsifying, moisturizing or drying, and adding color, flavor, and nutrients to the finished product. Eggs also may be used to retard crystallization in some frostings. Eggs in custard give structure and color.

Extracts: Concentrated flavorings that come from different foods and plants. Some are made by distilling fruits, seeds or leaves, anise, vanilla, peppermint, and almond extracts are made this way.

Filling: Frosting, preserves, or pudding that's spread between cake layers and holds them together.

Flan: A custard baked in a mold lined with caramelized sugar, chilled, and then unmolded.

Folding: Process whereby one ingredient or mixture is added to another, using a large metal spoon or spatula. Gentle process that often keeps mixed air fluffed throughout a mixture.

Fold In: To gently combine a heavier mixture with a more delicate substance such as beaten egg whites or whipped cream without causing a loss of air.

Garnishing: Presentation process whereby the appearance, flavor, and texture of a dish is enhanced with edible decorations.

Gelatin: Transparent protein, made from animal bones and tissue, which melts in hot liquid and forms a jelly when cold. Used for sweet and savory dishes. Available as unflavored and fruit-flavored. They are not interchangeable.

Icing: Sweet coating for cakes and pastries most often sugar-based and flavored; is it icing or frosting? It is both. Icing is a more professional term used when talking about frosting that is stiffer and pipes well. Frosting is considered homespun or creamier and softer.

Macadamia Nut: Also known as the Queensland nut. A fleshy white nut with a coconut-like flavor. In Asia, it is used in savory soups and stews. In the United States, the macadamia is used mostly in sweets. The nuts have an extremely high fat content.

Macaroon: A cookie made of eggs (usually whites) and almond paste or coconut.

Meringue: Beaten foam of egg whites and sugar, can be used as a pie topping, to lighten other mixtures and, after being baked to a crisp layer or shell, as the foundation of various cakes and desserts. Simple, uncooked meringue is made by beating egg whites, then beating in the sugar until very stiff, shiny peaks form. Cooked meringue is more stable. Two forms are: Swiss meringue egg whites and sugar heated over simmering water, then beaten until long, tall peaks form and the meringue is cold; Italian meringue, sugar syrup cooked to the firm-ball stage, beaten into whipped egg whites, then whipped until cold.

Mix: To stir in circles with a wooden spoon until ingredients are distributed evenly and there are no clumps of one ingredient. Or to combine with an electric mixer on low speed.

Nutmeg: Oval-shaped, brown, wrinkly seed of the nutmeg tree. When grated, it is primarily utilized in sweet and savory dishes, including cakes, custards, soufflés, meatballs, and soups.

Parchment Paper: A silicon-based paper that can withstand high heat. Often used to prepare sugar and chocolate confections because they do not stick to the paper at all. Parchment paper may be reused several times.

Peaks: When the beaters are lifted from egg whites or whipped cream peaks are briefly formed, but they do not hold their shape.

Peanut: Ground nut, eaten plain or roasted. Used to make peanut butter and oils.

Preheat: To heat oven to desired temperature before putting food in to bake. With most ovens, it takes from 15 to 20 minutes.

Pudding: Baked or boiled sweet dessert.

Puree: To reduce the pulp of cooked fruit and vegetables to a smooth and thick liquid by straining or blending.

Refrigerate: To chill in the refrigerator until a mixture is cool or a dough is firm.

Ricotta: Soft, unripened curded cheese. Ricotta is the

byproduct of whey that formulates during cheese processing. Sweet in flavor and grainy in texture. Often utilized in Italian sweets and pasta stuffings.

Salt: Common salt is a rock, the only one we eat (an inorganic mineral composed of 40 percent sodium and 60 percent chloride, joined by one of the strongest chemical unions there is, an ionic bond). One of the four elemental components of taste, along with sweet, sour, and bitter. Salt sharpens and pulls together other tastes. It comes from two primary sources; mines on land and water from the sea. Salt is also essential to our health. Without it, our cells cannot function properly and if we do not get enough of it, we will crave it until our physical need is satisfied.

Shortening: (1) Any fat used in baking to tenderize the product by shortening gluten strands. (2) A white, tasteless, solid fat that has been formulated for baking or deep-frying.

Softened: Margarine, butter, ice cream, or cream cheese that is in a state soft enough for easy blending, but not melted.

Soufflé: A baked dish containing whipped egg whites, which cause the dish to rise during baking.

Springform Pan: Baking tin with hinged sides, held together by a metal clamp or pin, which is opened to release the cake or pie cooked inside of it.

Stiff peaks: When the beaters are lifted from the egg whites, peaks are formed that hold their shape. When egg whites have reached the stiff peak stage, they are opaque, thick, and shiny, or glossy.

Stir: To move spoon in circular motion to incorporate ingredients. Usually refers to combining liquids or melted ingredients. To stir ingredients cooking on the stove top, use a wooden spoon and stir from the bottom of the pan to prevent scorching. Stirring helps to cool a mixture and evenly distribute the heat.

Strain: To pass through a strainer, sieve or cheesecloth to break down or remove solids or impurities.

Sweeteners: Any food that adds a sweet flavor to foods.

Sweet Almonds: These are used in cooking and can be eaten raw (either blanched without skins or with skins).

Toasting Nuts: Process whereby heat brings the oils closer to the surface of the nut which brings out more flavor. Method is useful in low-fat cooking in order to use fewer nuts. Toasting also makes removing the skins off of nuts easier.

Torte: Eastern European word for various types of cakes, usually layer cakes; meringue type dessert, usually rich in eggs and nuts.

Truffle: A French chocolate confection resembling a real truffle; small, round with a rough texture. A truffle is where ganache or other filling are enclosed by tempered chocolate and dusted with cocoa powder, confectioners' sugar, or chopped nuts; the essence of ganache.

Unsweetened Chocolate: Chocolate with no added sugar and is generally composed of 55 percent cocoa butter and 45 percent chocolate mass from the bean. Produces an intense chocolate flavor that must be tempered by sugar and other ingredients.

Walnut: Native to Asia and grow on walnut trees inside green pods which turn brown and wood like when dried.

Water Bath: Preparation method of gently cooking delicate foods such as custards on the stove top or in the oven by placing small cooking bowls, tins or pans in a larger pan partially filled with water.

Whip: To beat rapidly with a wire whisk or electric mixer to incorporate air into a mixture to lighten and increase the volume of the mixture.

Whipping: Preparation method whereby an item is mixed until frothy and creamy in consistency.

Whisk: A mixing tool designed so its many strands of looped wire make it effective for beating and adding air during preparation.

White Chocolate: Does not contain any chocolate. It is derived from cocoa butter, which produces a faint chocolate flavor. The cocoa butter is blended with milk and sugar to form the creamy confection, which is used for both eating and cooking.

Zest: Colored, oily outer skin of citrus fruit that, when grated or peeled, is used to flavor foods and liquids. The rind of citrus fruits such as orange, grapefruit, lime, and lemon.

APPENDIX B:
Calculating Carbohydrates

You can calculate the net carb value of any recipe by subtracting the grams of fiber, sugar alcohols, and glycerin from the number of carbohydrate grams.

EXAMPLE
40 Carbohydrates

5 Sugar Alcohols

10 Fibers

40 – 5 – 10 = 25 NET CARBS

NET CARB COUNT ON BAKING INGREDIENTS

Butter, Salted
Net Carbohydrate 0.14
  per cup

Butter, Unsalted
Net Carbohydrate 0.14
  per cup

Egg
Net Carbohydrate 0.14
  per egg

Egg Whites
Net Carbohydrate 0.23
  per cup

Egg Yolks
Net Carbohydrate 1.16
  per cup

Cream Cheese
Net Carbohydrate 0.06
  per ounce

Heavy Whipping Cream
Net Carbohydrate 0.03
  per fluid ounce

Ricotta Cheese
Net Carbohydrate 0.66
  per cup

Half and Half Cream
Net Carbohydrate 0.04
  per fluid ounce

Sour Cream
Net Carbohydrate 0.05
  per cup

Whipped topping
Net Carbohydrate 0.20
  per cup

Table Salt
Net Carbohydrate 0.00
  per teaspoon

Vanilla extract, imitation, alcohol
Net Carbohydrate 0.00 per
  teaspoon

Vanilla extract, imitation, no alcohol
Net Carbohydrate 0.60
  per teaspoon

Vanilla extract, pure, alcohol
Net Carbohydrate 0.25
  per teaspoon

Vanilla extract, pure, no alcohol
Net Carbohydrate 0.53
  per teaspoon

Ground Nutmeg
Net Carbohydrate 0.63
  per teaspoon

Cinnamon
Net Carbohydrate 0.05
  per teaspoon

Unsweetened Cocoa Powder
Net Carbohydrate 0.09 per
  tablespoon

Cooking Oil (Corn, Vegetable, or Light-Flavored Oil)
Net Carbohydrate 0.00 per cup

Blackberries (fresh)
Net Carbohydrate 5.04 per cup

Raspberries (fresh)
Net Carbohydrate 5.44 per cup

Strawberries (sliced)
Net Carbohydrate 7.24 per cup

Blueberries (fresh)
Net Carbohydrate 4.24 per cup

Banana (sliced)
Net Carbohydrate 13.34
  per cup

Walnuts (raw) (whole)
Net Carbohydrate 8.05 per cup

Pecans (raw) (chopped)
Net Carbohydrate 9.5 per cup

Brazil Nuts (raw) (chopped)
Net Carbohydrate 10.05
  per cup

Macadamia (raw) (whole)
Net Carbohydrate 11.05
  per cup

Almonds (raw) (sliced)
Net Carbohydrate 10.09
  per cup

Baking Soda
Net Carbohydrate 0.00
  per teaspoon

Baking Powder
Net Carbohydrate 0.00
  per teaspoon

White All Purpose
Net Carbohydrate 92.78
  per cup

Granulated Refined Sugar
Net Carbohydrate 99.91
  per cup

Unsweetened Baking Chocolate
Net Carbohydrate 0.26
  per ounce or 1 square

Peanut Butter (sugar-free smooth)
Net Carbohydrate 5.29 per
  2 tablespoons

Substitutions and Measurements

SUBSTITUTIONS

Almond Flour
Instead of almond flour, you can use ground almonds in a food processor worked to a powder.

Oat Flour
This flour can be substituted with protein powder.

Hazelnut Syrup
If you can't find hazelnut syrup, take 2 cups of raw hazelnuts; puree them in a food processor. Add 1/4 cup of artificial sweetener and 2 1/2 cups of water and boil on high heat for 10 minutes.

Eggs
Eggs can be substituted with Egg Beaters.

Espresso
Espresso can be substituted with strong coffee.

Pumpkin Spice
You can use All Spice as an alternative.

Lemon Juice
Imitation lemon juice will work as well. Use 1/2 the amount the recipe calls for.

Flaxseed Meal
Flaxseed meal can be substituted for almond flour or wheat flour.

Vanilla Whey Powder
The only other alternative is vanilla protein powder.

Half and Half Cream
Half and Half Cream is sometimes known as Light Cream. If you cannot find that, you can substitute heavy cream instead.

Nuts
(Walnuts, pecans, peanuts, macadamia, or Brazil nuts) Throughout all the recipes, you can change the nuts to any you desire.

MEASUREMENTS

Pound, cups, tablespoon, and teaspoon conversions assume the base weight-volume of water

1 pound = 2 cups

1 ounce = 2 tablespoons

1 tablespoon = 3 teaspoons = 0.5 oz = 15 grams

1 teaspoon = 0.17 oz = 5 grams

pinch is less than 1/8 teaspoon

dl = deciliter = 1/10 of a liter = 1/2 cup

Cake Flour   3 7/8 ounces = 1 cup

Bread Flour   4 1/4 ounces = 1 cup

Granulated Sugar   7 ounces = 1 cup

Confectioners' Sugar   5 ounces = 1 cup

Baking Powder   1/8 ounce = 1 teaspoon

Baking Soda   1/6 ounce = 1 teaspoon

Cream of Tartar   1/8 ounce = 1 teaspoon

Cinnamon   1/2 ounce = 6 teaspoons

Salt   1 ounce = 6 teaspoons

Butter   7 3/4 ounces = 1 cup

Hydrogenated Shortening   6 3/4 ounces = 6 teaspoons

Molasses 11 ounces = 1 cup

Honey 12 ounces = 1 cup

Eggs (whole) 5 = 1 cup

Egg Whites 8 = 1 cup

Egg Yolks 12 = 1 cup

Shredded Coconut 3 1/2 ounces = 1 cup

Ground Nuts 4 1/4 ounces = 1 cup

Nut pieces 4 ounces = 1 cup

Melted Chocolate 8 1/2 ounces = 1 cup

Cocoa 3 1/2 ounces = 1 cup

Gelatin 5 1/2 ounces = 1 cup

WEIGHT-VOLUME OF:

Flour 1 pound = 3 1/2 cups

Sugar 1 pound = 2 1/4 cups

ABBREVIATION CHART

c = cup

t = tsp = teaspoon

T = tbsp = tablespoon

C = Celsius

F = Fahrenheit

g = gr = gram

kg = kilogram

METRIC CONVERSION CHART

US	CANADIAN	AUSTRALIAN
1/4 tsp	1 mL	1 ml
1/2 tsp	2 mL	2 ml
1 tsp	5 mL	5 ml
1 Tbl	15 mL	20 ml

1/4 cup	50 mL	60 ml
1/3 cup	75 mL	80 ml
1/2 cup	125 mL	125 ml
2/3 cup	150 mL	170 ml
3/4 cup	175 mL	190 ml
1 cup	250 mL	250 ml
1 quart	1 liter	1 litre

WEIGHT

1 ounce	30 grams	30 grams
2 ounce	55 grams	60 grams
3 ounce	85 grams	90 grams
4 ounce	115 grams	125 grams
8 ounce	225 grams	225 grams
16 ounce	455 grams	500 grams (1/2 kilogram)

Temperatures

FAHRENHEIT	CELSIUS
32 degrees	0 degrees
212 degrees	100 degrees
250 degrees	120 degrees
275 degrees	140 degrees
300 degrees	150 degrees
325 degrees	160 degrees
350 degrees	180 degrees
375 degrees	190 degrees
400 degrees	200 degrees
425 degrees	220 degrees
450 degrees	230 degrees
475 degrees	240 degrees
500 degrees	260 degrees

Index

A
abbreviation chart, 150
almonds, 136
    Almond Delight Spritz Cookies, 6
    Almond Mousse, 90
    Almond Spring Cookies, 8
    Almond Whisper Cake, 28
    Autumn Cheesecake, 52–53
    Chocolate Cheesecake, 54–55
    Chocolate Orange Cheesecake, 56–57
    Eggnog Cheesecake Tart with Chocolate Crust, 78–79
    Low Carb Protein Bars, 19
    New York Style Cheesecake, 40–41
    Peanut Butter Cheesecake, 46–47
    Pumpkin Cheesecake, 42–43
    Strawberry Cheesecake, 44–45
    Strawberry Key Lime Cheesecake, 48–49

B
baking powder, 136
baking sheet, 136
baking soda, 136
bananas
    Banana Cake, 25
    Banana Ice Cream, 129
    Chocolate Cream Custard, 96
batter, 137
beating, 137
bitter almonds, 137
blend, 137
blueberries
    Berry Coconut Crème Pie, 67
    Blueberry Ice Cream, 125
    Blueberry Muffins, 34
    White Berry Cream Dessert, 94
boiling, 137
butterscotch
    Butterscotch Crème Pie, 64–65

C
cakes, 137
cakes and muffins
    Almond Whisper Cake, 28
    Banana Cake, 25
    Blueberry Muffins, 34
    Chocolate Cake Supreme, 26
    Chocolate Lovers Sponge, 37
    Chocolate Peanut Butter Cake, 30
    Coffee Cake Delight, 27
    Davenport Lemon Sponge, 36
    Faux Bran Muffins, 35
    Pound Cake, 24
    Pumpkin Pudding Cakes, 31
    Pumpkin Spice Cake with Cream Cheese Frosting, 32–33
    Sour Cream Occasion Cake, 29
cappuccino, 137
carbohydrates, 137–138
carbohydrates, calculating, 146–147
cheesecakes
    Autumn Cheesecake, 52–53
    Bake-Free Cherry Cheesecake, 39
    Caramel Pecan Cheesecake, 58
    Chocolate Cheesecake, 54–55
    Chocolate Orange Cheesecake, 56–57
    New York Style Cheesecake, 40–41
    Peanut Butter Cheesecake, 46–47
    Pumpkin Cheesecake, 42–43
    Quick Plain Cheesecake, 50
    Quick Plain Chocolate Cheesecake, 51
    Strawberry Cheesecake, 44–45
    Strawberry Key Lime Cheesecake, 48–49
chilling, 138
chocolate
    Cherry Squares, 115
    Chocolate Cake Supreme, 26
    Chocolate Cheesecake, 54–55
    Chocolate Chip Cookie, 2–3
    Chocolate Coconut Crunch Cups, 120
    Chocolate Crème Pie, 63
    Chocolate Frosting for Cakes or Cupcakes, 134
    Chocolate Joles, 121
    Chocolate Lovers Sponge, 37
    Chocolate Orange Cheesecake, 56–57
    Chocolate Peanut Butter Cake, 30

Chocolate Pecan le Torte, 75

Chocolate Topping, 132

Chocolate Torte, 76

Coffee Cake Delight, 27

Cream Cheese Chocolate Squares, 108

Dipping Chocolate, 135

Eggnog Cheesecake Tart with Chocolate Crust, 78–79

Frozen Chocolatesicles, 130

Guilt-Free Fudge, 100

Low Carb Chocolate Protein Bars, 17

Low Carb Cinnamon Bars, 18

Low Carb Peanut Butter Bars, 16

Macadamia Nut Chocolate Melt-A-Ways, 110

Mint Chocolate Delights, 113

Nutty Peanut Butter Fudge, 101

Peanut Butter Cup Poppers, 106

Peanut Butter Delights, 114

Peanut Butter Squares, 109

White Chocolate Fudge Dreams, 102

chocolate chips

Chocolate Chip Cookies, 2–3

chop, 138

cocoa powder, 138

coconut

Berry Coconut Crème Pie, 67

Chocolate Coconut Crunch Cups, 120

Cocoa Peanut Butter Truffles, 112

Coconut Peanut Butter Truffles, 119

Hazelnut Truffle Bites, 111

Macaroon Cookies, 7

Piña Colada Tea Cookies, 11

Victoria's Chews, 14

White Berry Cream Dessert, 94

combine, 138

cookies and bars

Almond Delight Spritz Cookies, 6

Almond Spring Cookies, 8

Chocolate Chip Cookies, 2–3

Hazelnut Mini Diamonds, 22

Lemon Meringue Bars, 20

Low Carb Chocolate Protein Bars, 17

Low Carb Cinnamon Bars, 18

Low Carb Peanut Butter Bars, 16

Low Carb Protein Bars, 19

Macadamia Nut Cheese Cookies, 21

Macaroon Cookies, 7

Peanut Butter Cookies, 5

Peanut Butter Patties, 15

Pecan Macaroons, 10

Pecan Sandies, 9

Piña Colada Tea Cookies, 11

Raspberry Wafer Cookies, 4

Sugar Cookies, 12

Victoria's Chews, 14

Walnut Cookies, 13

cooking spray, 138

cooling rack, 138

cream cheese

Autumn Cheesecake, 52–53

Bake-Free Cherry Cheesecake, 39

Butterscotch Crème Pie, 64–65

Caramel Pecan Cheesecake, 58

Chocolate Cheesecake, 54–55

Chocolate Cream Custard, 96

Chocolate Crème Pie, 63

Chocolate Frozen Drops, 107

Chocolate Joles, 121

Chocolate Meal Shake, 105

Chocolate Orange Cheesecake, 56–57

Cream Cheese Chocolate Squares, 108

Custard Pecan Pie, 70–71

Eggnog Cheesecake Tart with Chocolate Crust, 78–79

Eggnog Mousse, 95

Macadamia Nut Cheese Cookies, 21

Macadamia Vanilla Cheese Pie, 72–73

New York Style Cheesecake, 40–41

Oreo Mousse, 91

Peanut Butter Cheesecake, 46–47

Peanut Butter Squares, 109

Pumpkin Cheesecake, 40–41

Pumpkin Pudding Cakes, 31

Pumpkin Spice Cake with Cream Cheese Frosting, 32–33

Quick Plain Cheesecake, 50

Quick Plain Chocolate Cheesecake, 51

Raspberry Wafer Cookies, 4
Sour Cream Occasion Cake, 29
Strawberry Cheesecake, 44–45
Strawberry Crème Pie, 68–69
Strawberry Key Lime Cheesecake, 48–49
Vanilla Crème Pie, 66
Vanilla Praline Pecan Torte, 77
White Berry Cream Dessert, 94
cream of tartar, 139
creaming, 138–139
crème brûlèe, 139
custard, 139
custards, flan, and mousse
Almond Mousse, 90
Banana Mousse Supreme, 89
Banana Spanish Flan, 86
Bread Pudding, 97
Chocolate Cream Custard, 96
Chocolate Spanish Flan, 85
Crème Brûlèe, 98
Egg Custard, 83
Eggnog Mousse, 95
Lemon Crème Mousse, 87
Oreo Mousse, 91
Raspberry Crème Mousse, 88
Spanish Flan, 84
Tapioca, 92
Tiramisù, 81
White Berry Cream Dessert, 94
White Chocolate Crème Mousse, 93
White Chocolate Mousse Trifle, 82
cut, 139
cut and fold, 139

D
deep-frying, 139
dessert, 139–140
dissolve, 140
double boiler, 140
dry ingredients, 140
dusting, 140

E
eggs, 140
extracts, 140

F
filling, 141
flan, 141
folding, 141
fudge, chocolate, and candy
Brownie Bites, 104
Cappuccino Hazelnut Candy, 117
Cherry Squares, 115
Chocolate Coconut Crunch Cups, 120
Chocolate Doughnut Fritters, 118
Chocolate Frozen Drops, 107
Chocolate Joles, 121
Chocolate Meal Shake, 105
Chocolate Raspberry Truffles, 110
Cocoa Peanut Butter Truffles, 112
Coconut Peanut Butter Truffles, 119
Cream Cheese Chocolate Squares, 108
Guilt-Free Fudge, 100
Hazelnut Truffle Bites, 111
Little Boo's Brownies, 103
Macadamia Nut Chocolate Melt-A-Ways, 116
Mint Chocolate Delights, 113
Nutty Peanut Butter Fudge, 101
Peanut Butter Cup Poppers, 106
Peanut Butter Delights, 114
Peanut Butter Squares, 109
White Chocolate Fudge Dreams, 102

G
garnishing, 141
gelatin, 141

H
hazelnuts
Cappuccino Hazelnut Candy, 117
Hazelnut Mini Diamonds, 22

I
ice cream and frozen treats
Banana Ice Cream, 129
Blueberry Ice Cream, 125
Chocolate Ice Cream, 127
Cinnamon Ice Cream, 126
Frozen Chocolatesicles, 130

Peanut Butter Ice Cream, 128
Simple Vanilla Ice Cream, 123
Strawberry Ice Cream, 124
icing, 141

L
lemons
Davenport Lemon Sponge, 36
Lemon Crème Mousse, 87
Lemon Meringue Bars, 20

M
macadamia nuts, 141
Macadamia Nut Cheese Cookies, 21
Macadamia Nut Chocolate
Melt-A-Ways, 116
Macadamia Vanilla Cheese Pie,
72–73
macaroon, 141
measurements, 149–150
meringue, 141–142
metric conversion chart, 150–151
mix, 142

N
nutmeg, 142

P
parchment paper, 142
peaks, 142
peanut, 142
peanut butter
Chocolate Frozen Drops, 107
Chocolate Meal Shake, 105
Chocolate Peanut Butter Cake, 30
Cocoa Peanut Butter Truffles, 112
Coconut Peanut Butter Truffles, 119
Hazelnut Truffle Bites, 111
Low Carb Peanut Butter Bars, 16
Low Carb Protein Bars, 19
Nutty Peanut Butter Fudge, 101
Peanut Butter Cheesecake, 46–47
Peanut Butter Cookies, 5
Peanut Butter Cup Poppers, 106
Peanut Butter Delights, 114
Peanut Butter Ice Cream, 128
Peanut Butter Patties, 15

Peanut Butter Squares, 109
Silk Peanut Butter Pie, 60–61
Victoria's Chews, 14
pecans
Caramel Pecan Cheesecake, 58
Chocolate Pecan le Torte, 75
Custard Pecan Pie, 70–71
Low Carb Peanut Butter Bars, 16
Nutty Peanut Butter Fudge, 101
Pecan Macaroons, 10
Pecan Sandies, 9
Pumpkin Pecan Pie, 74
Vanilla Praline Pecan Torte, 77
pies and tarts
Berry Coconut Crème Pie, 67
Butterscotch Crème Pie, 64–65
Chocolate Crème Pie, 63
Chocolate Pecan le Torte, 75
Chocolate Torte, 76
Custard Pecan Pie, 70–71
Eggnog Cheesecake Tart with
Chocolate Crust, 78–79
Macadamia Vanilla Cheese Pie,
72–73
Pumpkin Pecan Pie, 74
Pumpkin Pie Dessert Cups, 62
Silk Peanut Butter Pie, 60–61
Strawberry Crème Pie, 68–69
Vanilla Crème Pie, 66
Vanilla Praline Pecan Torte, 77
preheat, 142
pudding, 142
pumpkin
Autumn Cheesecake, 52–53
Pumpkin Cheesecake, 40–41
Pumpkin Pecan Pie, 74
Pumpkin Pie Dessert Cups, 62
Pumpkin Pudding Cakes, 31
Pumpkin Spice Cake with Cream
Cheese Frosting, 32–33
pumpkin pie dessert cups, 62
puree, 142

R
raspberries
Chocolate Raspberry Truffles, 110
Raspberry Crème Mousse, 88

Raspberry Wafer Cookies, 4
White Berry Cream Dessert, 94
refrigerate, 142
ricotta, 142–143

S
salt, 143
shortening, 143
softened, 143
soufflé, 143
sour cream
    Caramel Pecan Cheesecake, 58
    Chocolate Cheesecake, 54–55
    Chocolate Orange Cheesecake, 56–57
    Eggnog Cheesecake Tart with Chocolate Crust, 78–79
    Pumpkin Pecan Pie, 74
    Quick Plain Cheesecake, 50
    Quick Plain Chocolate Cheesecake, 51
    Sour Cream Occasion Cake, 29
    Strawberry Cheesecake, 44–45
    Vanilla Praline Pecan Torte, 77
springform pan, 143
stiff peaks, 143
stir, 143
strain, 144
strawberry
    Berry Coconut Crème Pie, 67
    Lemon Crème Mousse, 87
    Strawberry Cheesecake, 44–45
    Strawberry Crème Pie, 68–69
    Strawberry Ice Cream, 124
    Strawberry Key Lime Cheesecake, 48–49
    Vanilla Praline Pecan Torte, 77
    White Berry Cream Dessert, 94
    White Chocolate Mousse Trifle, 82
susbstitutions, 148–149
sweet almonds, 144
sweeteners, 144

T
temperature conversion chart, 151
tiramisù, 81
toasting nuts, 144
toppings and frostings
    Chocolate Frosting for Cakes or Cupcakes, 134
    Chocolate Topping, 132
    Dipping Chocolate, 135
    Vanilla Frosting for Cakes or Cupcakes, 133
torte, 144
truffle, 144

U
unsweetened chocolate, 144

W
walnuts, 144
    Banana Cake, 25
    Brownie Bites, 104
    Little Boo's Brownies, 103
    Low Carb Cinnamon Bars, 18
    Walnut Cookies, 13
water bath, 144
weight-volume of, 150
whipping, 145
whisk, 145
white chocolate, 145
    White Chocolate Crème Mousse, 93
    White Chocolate Mousse Trifle, 82

Z
zest, 145